RELIGIOUS SOCIALISATION

10. J.A. van der Ven, Entwurf einer empirischen Theologie, Kampen/ Weinheim, 1990.
11. B.J. Groen, Ter genezing van ziel en lichaam. De viering van het olie-sel in de Grieks-orthodoxe kerk, Kampen/Weinheim, 1990.
12. C.A.M. Hermans, Wie werdet Ihr die Gleichnisse verstehen? Kampen/Weinheim, 1990
13. J.A. van der Ven & H.G. Ziebertz (Hrsg), Paradigmenentwicklung in der Praktischen Theologie, Kampen / Weinheim, 1993.
14. J. Siemerink, Voorgaan in de liturgie. Vorming van vrijwilligers, Kampen/Weinheim, 1993.
15. H.G. Heimbrock, Gottesdienst: Spielraum des Lebens. Sozial- und kulturwissenschaftliche Analysen zum Ritual in praktisch-theologi-schem Interesse, Kampen/Weinheim, 1993.
16. R. Jeurissen, Peace and Religion. An Empirical-Theological Study of the Motivational Effects of Religious Peace Attitudes on Peace Action, Kampen/Weinheim, 1993.
17. H.-G. Ziebertz, Sexualpädagogik in gesellschaftlichem Kontext. Studien zur Konzeptentwicklung katholischer Sexualerziehung, Kampen/Weinheim, 1993.
18. Fred van Iersel & Marijke Spanjersberg, Vrede leren in de kerk, Kampen/Weinheim, 1993.
19. Frank Kwakman & Jan van Oers, Het geloof in de katholieke basis-school. Over legitimaties voor de katholieke basisschool in een multi-etnische en geseculariseerde samenleving, Kampen/Weinheim 1993.
20. B. Biemans & J.A. van der Ven, Religie in fragmenten. Een onder-zoek onder studenten, Kampen/Weinheim, 1994.
21 E. Henau & R.J. Schreiter (eds.), Religious Socialisation, Kampen/ Weinheim, 1995.
22 J.A. van der Ven & H.-G. Zieberts (Hrsg.), Religiöser Pluralismus und Interreligiöses Lernen, Kampen/Weinheim,1994.

Herausgegeben von
H.F. Rupp, A.H.M. Scheer, J.A. van der Ven, H.-G. Ziebertz.

E. Henau

R.J. Schreiter

C.A.M. Hermans

H.-G. Ziebertz

J.A. van der Ven

A. de Jong

RELIGIOUS SOCIALISATION

E. Henau & R.J. Schreiter (eds.)

DEUTSCHER STUDIEN VERLAG
KOK

CIP-GEGEVENS KONINKLIJKE BIBLIOTHEEK, DEN HAAG

©1995 J.H. Kok Publishing House – Kampen/The Netherlands
Deutscher Studien Verlag – Weinheim/Germany
Cover Design by Atelier Warminski
ISBN Kok 90 390 0064 6
ISBN DSV 3-89271-541-6
NUGI 632

Contents

Contributors

Preface

This volume is the result of an international congress held on the 25th of May 1993 at the University for Theological and Pastoral Studies (UTP) in Heerlen, the Netherlands.
The topic of the congress was 'the transgenerational mediation of faith'.
For more then 1900 years Christian faith has been passed from generation to generation and each generation experienced his own difficulties. At present, however, probably for the first time on a large scale, fundamental questions are being raised. How can one generation's particular expression of the Christian faith be passed on to the next generation within our changing society? Or is this possible at all in these times of secularisation?

This volume incorporates the lectures of Professor Schreiter (Chicago), Professor Henau (Heerlen/Louvain) and Professor van der Ven (Nijmegen) on several aspects of this theme given at the congress. In addition, it contains articles written by Professor Hermans (Nijmegen), Dr. de Jong (Heerlen) and Dr. Ziebertz (Nijmegen) who were inspired by the congress.

Theologians and those interested in pastoral theology will find this volume helpful in gaining a clear view of the problems of and prospects for the mediation of the Christian faith and aspects of the Christian tradition at the end of the twentieth century.

We wish to express our thanks to Frank van Gerven, principal organiser of the congress. Without his help this volume would not exist.

Heerlen, summer 1994

Ernest Henau
Robert J. Schreiter

I The Broken Pact between the Generations

E. Henau

More than half a century ago, T.S. Eliot was invited by the Masters and Fellows of Corpus Christi College, Cambridge, to give three lectures on the idea of continuity of Christian tradition in a liberal society. In these lectures which afterwards were published under the title The idea of a Christian Society, Eliot took up the challenge of formulating an answer to the problem, a problem that has become more pressing ever since. He argued that liberalism advocates the cause of tolerance and draws a distinction between public morality and private religious conviction as two alternatives of an overall view of society. This leads to the general conception that a society, in which religious conviction is considered a private matter, poses no threat to christian faith and practice. On the contrary, it clears the way for different christian denominations to live together peacefully. Eliot did not deny that there is some practical truth in this idea, but he maintained that liberal society containes something that goes against religious neutrality. He wrote: 'The liberal notion that religion ... (is) a matter of private belief and of conduct in private life, and that there is no reason why Christians should not be able to accomodate themselves to any world which treats them good-naturally, is becoming less and less tenable.'[1] The new public moralty, he argued, is dominated by a purely mechanical notion of freedom, the primary goal of which is to put into effect prosperity in this world for the individual or for the group. This definition of freedom and the 'acquisitive, utilitarian morality' it encourages are thoroughly opposed to the Christian view of life.

Imperceptively Christian virtues are being restricted and curtailed in people's lives. The prevailing public morality creates 'the compulsion to live in such a way that Christian behaviour is only possible in a restricted number of situations'.[2] Christian hope is crippled and eventually converted into 'the (secular) notion of getting on to which the alternative is a hopeless apathy'.[3] Furthermore, the driving force of liberalism is directed toward the dissolution of religious and social traditions. 'For it is something which tends to release energy rather than accumulate it, to relax, rather than to fortify. It is a movement not so much defined by its end, as by its starting point, away

---

1. T.S. Eliot, Christianity and Culture, New York, 1940, 17.
2. Ibid., 24.
3. Ibid., 16.

9

from, rather than towards, something definite.'[4] Liberalism 'redefines all other traditions as matters of individual or group preference'.[5] It destroys 'traditional social habits of people' and dissolves 'their natural collective consciousness into individual constituents'.[6] In such an environment Christian faith gradually loses its impact on the world of people's imagination. No longer does it give inspiration to hope and to a vision of the supreme good. The end result is the creation of 'bodies of men and women – of all classes – detached from tradition, alienated from religion and susceptible to mass suggestion'.[7]

From the point of view of Christian faith, Eliot says, the problem is no longer that of 'a minority in a society of individuals holding an alien belief. It is the problem constitued by our implication in a network of institutions from which we cannot dissociate ourselves: institutions the operation of which appears no longer neutral, but non-Christian'.[8] Even the distinction between private and secular public morality seems no longer to be maintained in the life of many Christians whose private morality simply reproduces the new public ethos. 'And as for the Christian who is not conscious of this dilemma in living in such a culture – and he is in the majority – he is becoming more and more de-christianized by all sorts of unconscious pressure: paganism holds al the most valuable advertising space.'[9] This situation, says Eliot, has become so typical that 'anything like Christian traditions transmitted from generation to generation within the family must disappear, and the small body of Christians will consist entirely of adult recruits.'[10]

That which Eliot announced more than fifty years ago is happening today in front of our very eyes. During ages a sort of pact existed between the generations. Each generation was aware of the fact that it owed its living space to the previous one. For that reason care was taken of the possibilities of life of the next generation. People planted trees even in the knowledge that they would never harvest the fruits. A similar pact existed in matters of religion as well. Parents subjected their children to the rites they themselves had been subjected to. Perhaps they did not clearly percieve what was the purpose of all this. But they considered the risk of breaking the religious pact between the generations to be too high. Such a pact has always to do with

---

4. Ibid., 15.
5. Cfr. Alasdair Mc Intyre, Whose Justice? Whose Rationality?, Notre Dame, 1988, Chapter 17.
6. Eliot, p. 16.
7. Ibid., 21.
8. Ibid., 22.
9. Ibid., 22.
10. Ibid., 11.

the transmission of possibilities of life. And it is of no crucial importance to the transmitter whether he or she believes in the reality of what is passed along as a possibility. Nor is the transmission inspired by any obligation that transcends the act of transmitting as such. In her memories Marguérite Yourcenar offered a splendid picture of how all this frequently resulted in a very formal religiosity.[11] She confronts us with a kind of Catholicism that was reduced to rites and customs, the inner side of which was completely eroded.[12]

This reference to Yourcenar makes it clear that the metaphor of the broken pact is indeed no more than a figure of speech. The phenomenon that Eliot pointed out, viz. the disappearance of christian traditions handed down from generation to generation, is no comet-like phenomenon suddenly making its appearance in the sky. It is not, as the metaphor of the broken pact might suggest, the result of a punctual decision. It is the end point of an evolution. There is indeed common agreement that the contemporary situation with regard to Christian faith is the outcome of a nummber of processes that began centuries ago. Two related tendencies, that reinforce each other, deserve to be singled out. First of all, there is the tendency to privatization that Eliot pointed out. It has its roots in the weakening of faith as an integrative force in society. When the wars of religion resulting from the Reformation had brought society on the verge of disaster, the idea arose that the only way to overcome the antagonism was to establish the organisation of society not on religious principles but on human nature and reason. Initially this view took root only in a small circle of intellectuals. Step by step, however, and in spite of resistance and struggle, it gained the upper hand until it became the generally accepted outlook in our days. Religion, in so far as it still counts for anything at all, is commonly considered a private matter. This tendency has been strengthened by another development. Since the industrial revolution our society has evolved toward an ever increasing differentiation. In order to understand what is meant by this we must take a look back at the earlier agrarian society. There, a person's life was not segmented. The extended family to which one belonged was at the same time a productive and a living community, i.e. a community in which people lived and worked together. Recreation and the rudimentary schooling which they needed were found locally, namely in the village of which the family formed an integral part. Religion, i.e. the Church, was the integrating factor in all this. Modern society, on the contrary, has originated from an ever progressing segmentation of life. This means that it now consists of a considerable number of seg-

---

11. M. Yourcenar, Archives du Nord, Paris, 1977.
12. Cfr. M. Yourcenar, Souvenirs pieux, Éd. Gallimard, 1974.

ments, such as the world of labour, of the media, of culture, education, economy, transport, health care, sports, entertainment, etc. All these segments have grown into relatively independant (sub)systems. One positive effect of this development (development toward liberal society in the sense Eliot gives that term) was that it liberated man from the social constraints and the moral fault-finding of traditional communities that were organized according to religious standards. Man has gained more freedom of movement. The other side of the medal is that thereby a burden is put on man that he is hardly able to bear. The various (sub)systems constantly challenge him to engage him/herself, to become a member, to participate, etc.

One became liable to so many demands, appeals, invitations etc. that one could not but try to keep one's distance. This attempt to be distant, to withdraw into the private sphere as a buffer-zone against a differentiated and demanding society was an absolute necessity for the individual, if one did not want to be swallowed up by all the various social fields of interest. The need for dissociating oneself was therefore also part of an elementary pattern of behaviour in our extremely complicated society. As in our industrialized society of today the Church is no longer an integrating factor, but a segment among segments (an institution among institutions), she shares in the dissociating behaviour that modern man develops in this society with its many competing factors.

This is why religion and church no longer can rely on 'the pressure of conformity'; something which once favoured (superficially at least) religious behaviour. The results of these desintegrative developments are well known and have been named: pluralisation, modernisation, individualisation and so on.

The question is of course – how to react to these developments. As we have already seen T.S. Eliot's answer was a renewed plea for 'the idea of a christian society'. He proposed that this should be cultivated, to render it accessible as an intellectual support in the inevitable future moment of cultural despair regarding all other means of action. He considered that the idea of a christian society still had a chance in England in view of the large number of christian societies in that land: state church included. 'It is my contention that we have to-day a culture which is mainly negative, but which, so far as it is positive, is stil Christian. I do not think that it can remain negative, because a negative culture has ceased to be efficient in a world where economic as well as spiritual forces are proving the efficiency of cultures which, even when pagan, are positive; and I believe that the choice before us is between the formation of a new Christian culture, and the acceptance of a pagan one. Both involve radical changes; but I believe that the majority of us, if we could be faced immediately with all the changes which will only be accomplished in several generations, would prefer Christianity'.[13]

Eliot's attraction to the idea of a christian society was certainly not prompted by a nostalgic hankering after 'the good old days', nor the wish that the church could once again play a powerful role in society. He also did not wish to propagate the idea of a christian society with church and religion defined as being the moral pillars of social order. 'What is worst of all', he wrote, 'is to advocate Christianity, not because it is true, but because it provides a foundation of morality, instead of showing the necessity of Christian morality from the truth of Christianity, is a very dangerous inversion; and we may reflect, that a good deal of the attention of totalitarian states has been devoted, with a steadiness of purpose not always found in democracies, to providing their national life with a foundation of morality'.[14]

Eliot supported the idea of a christian society because he had a high opinion of the social character of christianity and of the absolute necessity of a social incorporation of belief. This embodiment of faith should not be restricted to the church but rather extend to embrace society as a whole. This followed, in this opinion, from the belief in Trinity and Incarnation.[15] At the same time he warned against all forms of christian utopias. A christian society is exposed to decay and will always feel the need for reform. 'I have tried to restrict my ambition of a christian society', Eliot wrote, 'to a social minimum: to picture not a society of saints, but of ordinary men, of men whose Christianity is communal before being individual'.[16] Nonetheless doubts do arise regarding Eliot's sense of reality. His biographer, Ackroyd, writes: 'that The idea of a Christian society should make little appeal to the large majority of the intelligentia. But this volume received scarcely any warmer welcome from the Church. According to Ackroyd Eliot had little idea of 'the nature of English life; his grasp of it was theoretical rather than actual'.[17]

We have stated in detail Eliot's plea for a christian society, not because we are persuaded but rather because Eliot has, in a nutshell, formulated the central problem regarding the transmission of christian tradition in a liberal society: a problem that has become even more acute now that this is the only

---

13. Ibid., 13.
14. Ibid., 59.
15. This convictions not only present in The idea of a christian society; it is dicernible in his poetical works as well. See H. Servotte, De Four Quartets, vertaald, ingeleid en gecommentarieerd, Antwerpen / Amsterdam, 1974.
16. Eliot, 59.
17. P. Ackroyd, T.S.Eliot. A Life, New York, 1984, 251.

remaining social form. If this signifies, as Fukoyama thinks, that we are experiencing the end of history, I will not discuss at this point.[18] It seems to me in any case a strange idea that the human race, in the liberal structure of society, has reached a stage in its evolution where further development can not be attained. I am prepared to accept that we have at the present time no social alternative and that the continuity of christianity will need to be guaranteed in this structure, i.e., the liberal society. It is therefore not arrogant to think that the future of christianity will not be forged in the developing lands where it appears to enjoy greater vitality, but here. If the pluriform democratic form of government, based on science and on technology, should become the universal model, then the problems facing the transmission of faith will also be universal. The future will largely depend on if we will be able to overcome the, seemingly apparent, logical inconsistency of a number of contradictory premises in a sort of 'coincidentia oppositorum'. What are these contradictions?

1. – Everyone not possessing a fundamentalistic view of society will look on the pluriform democratic coexistence as being the best possible. This implies that religion is a private matter and no longer the integrating factor of society. On the other hand a believer will not readily accept that faith has no social consequences. The question to be faced is: how can one reconcile the notion that belief is a private matter with the necessity of translating his personal faith in social terms.

2. – Faith is intrinsic adherence; a free personal choice that cannot be enforced. On the other hand, faith is social behaviour. It wells up in confrontation with a tradition borne by a social group and requires structural plausibility. One is more than ever convinced of the truth of the old adage: 'Unus christianus nullus christianus'.

3. – Faith is a private matter but also feels the need to express itself according to the scholastic adage: 'bonum diffusivum sui'. Since it makes a claim to universality, Christianity cannot be but missionary. Otherwise it would abolish itself.

4. – Christian faith is no longer an integrating factor in our society and has lost its priviledged character. On the other hand it is at the same time the cultural ethical substrate of our civilisation and is not to be equated with other ideologies of religious forms.

Against this background we can now search for concepts to govern our actions. In the first place there is the idea, defended by Eliot, of the christian society. In the present circumstances, as we have already suggested, this is no more than a utopia and if Eliot were alive today he would more than

---

18.   Cfr. F. Fukoyama, The End of History and the Last Man, New York, 1992.

probably reject it. Even now it may well appeal to a number, although Eliot would not recognise himself in their expectations. It is not althogether impossible that the progressive erosion of social ethics will strengthen the conviction that collective values without religious roots have no future.

At the other end of the spectrum we find the idea of christianity as a cognitive minority with several variants; 'small herd', 'contrast group', 'Gideon's three hundred', 'critical spearhead'. It is worthy of note that these variants are to be found on both right and left wings and display in common opposition to the ruling culture. The right wing variants proceed from the basis that 'the truth' should be propagated without compromise and that 'wheat' must be separated from 'chaff'; and this without taking into account that this, for the gospel, is an eschatological activity. Some prefer to imagine that this is only a temporary situation, rather like an overwintering, after which inevitably a new spring will come. Still others consider the minority position to be the genuine mode of existence of the faithful; to be a small herd in the middle of a hostile or disinterested world.

Also on the left wing are some who are convinced that the church has no future other than a sort of contrast or alternative society which will oppose the ruling values and norms of the consumption economy. Here once again there are two groups; one which thinks in terms of the radical demands made by the gospel; that this is the real mode of existence for a christian society: a group which, just because of its critical social choices, will continue to occupy a minority position. The other group is convinced that a radical stance will in the long run serve to increase the church's attraction to those who at present either pass by indifferently of who have quietly absented.

We continue to chose for a combined strategy, with two characteristics which are, to a certain degree, complementary and so to realise the 'coincidentia oppositorum' about which we just spoke. On the one hand we must take care that christian belief remains accessible to forums of public discussion and on the other hand we should create, maintain and propagate what bishop Ernst calls 'milieus of faith', in which belief shows to be an attractive way of life. Where this is directed specifically at the transmission of faith, we launch a plea for mutually complementary priorities.
1) Christian participation in public debates in the media needs to be encouraged by means of an inventive preaching and inspired presentation of moral values and ways of life fired by the spirit of Christ.
2) Exertions made in recent times aimed at defining the place of religious instruction should be continued. It is essential to insist upon the necessity of knowledge of the christian faith for two purposes; on the one hand for cultivating knowledge of the jewish-christian tradition which forms the ethical foundation of our culture, and on the other hand to realise the possibility of

making responsible decisions concerning religion and christian belief.

3) It will also be necessary to realise 'a milieu of faith', composed of people who are convinced that christian belief, as a personal experience, is not just one dimension of life alongside others but the one, central dimension which governs all the rest. Such a milieu is not only important for the identity of christianity, it is an essential structure in the credibility of belief. In our society, belief is becoming less and less a cognitive process and increasingly attained through identification and witness.

4) This is why we need, in addition to the informative way of religious instruction and initiation in the sacraments, supplementation with the proven experience of the value of the christian way of life. This sort of experience is hardly possible in childhood and adolescense but comes more often in late youth and early adulthood. Traditional transfer of faith has thus changed from what J. Moingt called 'l'automaticité de la sacramentalisation' more and more to chosing and trying for oneself.

There are no magical solutions for the present pastoral problems. Should it be true that we are now confronted with a breakpoint in time, this implies that a new era awaits us, one in which christianity must again find a place. Not only will this need dedication and inventiveness but much patience. That is why I end this introduction with a reflection of Vaclav Havel, who once made an impressive plea for 'active waiting'. His description of his personal situation is equally applicable to ours: 'We must sow the seed patiently, and stubbornly continue to water the earth in which it is sown and then allow the plants their own time. We can no more fool a plant than we can fool history; but we can give it water. Patiently, every day. With understanding, with humility, and of cours also with love.'[19]

---

19.   'Le Monde' of 29th of october 1992.

II Faith Between the Risk Society and the Experience Society

Robert J. Schreiter

1. Elements in the Transgenerational Mediation of Faith

Issues about how to transmit Christian faith from one generation to the next confront every culture in every age. Human societies are dynamic and are always undergoing change in some measure. On the edge where the present meets the future that change can seem very rapid indeed. In retrospect, however, changes may take longer than was at first apparent. At any rate, the task of Christian ministry in each generation is to find the best possible ways of transmitting faith to the subsequent generation.

In contemporary Europe, this task is an extraordinarily challenging one. Western Europe, the cradle of Latin Christianity, is more deeply secularized than the societies in North America. Apart from the struggle with secularization in Europe, which has already been going on for a long time, new factors have to be taken into consideration. The new migration into Europe of economic and political refugees is reshaping European societies in ways yet to be understood. Guest workers, who once were thought to be but a temporary part of industrial societies, are beginning their third generation of presence in many countries.
Multicultural ministry and education are new areas for most of us, although research into multicultural education has already formed a fairly coherent body of literature. And finally, the end of the East-West division through the center of Europe has created enormous challenges for the western countries, especially Germany. Europe is trying to cope with all of this in the midst of a broader economic upheaval and communications revolution that is reordering the world in profound ways.[1]

It is in the midst of all of this that we are trying to discern how to transmit Christian faith to the next generation. Secularization, with its largely instrumental rationality appears opposed to any normative status that might be accorded to tradition. It is wedded to a view of progress that sees the past

---

1. I have tried to explore some of this in 'Multicultural Ministry: Theory, Practice, Theology,' New Theology Review 5(August, 1992) 6-19; 'Contextualization from a World Perspective,' Theological Education 29(Spring, 1993)forthcoming.

as increasingly obsolete and superceded. The church is seen as a relic of that past, whose outmoded ways and authoritarian stances make it irrelevant to contemporary society. The presence of many cultures in areas that heretofore were deemed monocultural[2] raises new questions about communication and intelligibility. And the renewed interaction between eastern and western Europe raises questions about what values undergird society. The push and pull of immigration, reunification, integration into a European community, and a global reordering of relationships create a special strain on meaning and identity formation at this point in our history.

To speak of transgenerational mediation of faith in this context, then, is a formidable challenge. My part of this task is to see how sociological research can shed light on the religious task: both the theological challenges of how we will formulate our faith for the sake of its transmission, and the pastoral challenges that are attendant upon it. What can be said about all of this in the short compass of this presentation will be limited and at times more suggestive or sketchy than fully developed. I try here to undertake three things. First of all, to look at some of the dimensions that constitute the transgenerational mediation of faith. Some of these dimensions arise out of a sociological frame of reference, others out of the theological. Then, the presentation turns to two visions of contemporary society, both based on research done in Germany: the 'risk society,' which explores how threats to our survival are being redistributed in postmodern society; and the 'experience society,' which looks at how economic abundance reshapes society. These names have been taken from two books that are so entitled, written by Ulrich Beck and Gerhard Schulze, respectively.[3] Each of these views of society will be looked at separately, but will be enhanced with data from other advanced industrial societies. The research seems to indicate that, even though advanced industrial societies arose out of distinctive histories and circumstances, and have had somewhat differing paths of development, the end result -at least for European and North American societies- show remarkable parallels. Within the look at both of these views of society, I will try to draw out of them the agenda they raise for the transmittal of faith, and then suggest what steps we might undertake to achieve our goal of fulfilling

---

2. See Klaus J. Bade, Deutsche im Ausland – Fremde in Deutschland (München: C.H. Beck, 1992).

3. Ulrich Beck, Risikogesellschaft: Auf dem Weg in eine andere Moderne (Frankfurt a.M.: Suhrkamp, 1986). Quotations here from the English edition Risk Society: Towards a New Modernity (London: Sage, 1992). Gerhard Schulze, Die Erlebnisgesellschaft: Zur Kultursoziologie der Gegenwart (Frankfurt: Campus, 1992).

the responsibility to 'pass on what has been handed down' to us.[4]

And so, on to the first part. We will explore here the significance of 'generation,' the dynamics of transmission, and what we hope to mediate – namely, Christian faith.

2. New Elements in Generation

How exactly to define a generation is always a delicate task. One can do this mathematically, in lots of twenty or thirty years, but that is somewhat artificial for our purposes. More frequently, generations are defined by events that have affected society profoundly. Thus, we speak of the generation born between the world wars, or the post-war generation, or the post-1968 generation. Speaking in this fashion is more useful for our discussion here, because it points to events that putatively have shaped the outlook of a given generation. The economic depression of the 1930's, the war, the cultural upheavals of the late 1960's – all have left their mark on the people who experienced them. But they are especially important to those people whose formative years, from middle childhood to late adolescence, coincided with these events. Thus we encounter people whom we say 'never really got over' the war or the sixties. What we mean by such a designation is that these crucial events remain normative for interpreting all new experience subsequent to that time. That often means a fixation with a powerful – and now past – period. But it also gives us a clue into how these people's mental universe is shaped.

This yields an important element for consideration. It was best expressed by sociologist Norman Ryder in a 1965 essay: 'In an epoch of change, each person is dominated by his birth date.'[5] Birthdate dominates, but it does not determine. Thus, those who came of age during the Second World War had a very short adolescence, whereas those who came of age in the late 1960's probably had an extended one. Birthdate does give us a benchmark by which to calculate which larger societal trends and events any given person or group would have had to encounter in their formative years. As we look further at the transmittal of faith, we need to ask the birthdate question.

Closely connected to birthdate as an important element is the concept of age cohort. Age cohort is a unit of measurement used by demographers. Its purpose is to discern societal trends on the basis of impact of age groups. The

---

4.   This was the finding of Ronald Inglehart, Culture Shift in Advanced Industrial Society (Princeton: Princeton University Press, 1990).
5.   Norman Ryder, 'The Cohort as a Concept in the Study of Social Change,' American Sociological Review 30(1965)843-861.

most studied of these age cohorts has been the post-war generation of 1946-1964, often called the 'baby boom' generation because of the large increase in the birthrate during that period.[6] In the United States, where much of the research has been done, it represents the largest age cohort in American history, and constitutes almost one-third of the entire population. Consequently, it is moving through history like 'a pig through a python,' to use the colorful phrase of one demographer. When they were children in the 1950's, the United States was preoccupied with childcare and building enough schools to educate them. By the mid-1960's, higher education was expanding to accommodate their entry into university, and the contradictions of the Vietnam War, their coming of age, and (for Roman Catholics) the aftermath of the Second Vatican Council made for a heady brew that bubbled over and changed society. All of this was fueled further by the political assassinations of the Kennedys and of Martin Luther King, Jr., the civil rights movement, and the growing feminist movement. This same group settled down in the seventies and into the eighties and dwelt on making money and self-realization. The research at this point in the 1990's points to an end to that narcissism and a concern for relationships and the larger world, as this group moves into middle age.

This group, and the cohort immediately behind it that is growing up in reaction to many of the baby boomers' excesses, constitute the cohorts on which we need to concentrate as we look at the matter of transmitting faith.[7] On the upper end, we have a group in their mid-forties, ripe for mid-life assessment of their values and orientation.

Values of transcendence, of personal and the universal, the quality of friendship and relationship, the quest for wisdom – all of these often happen at this time.[8] The middle group are having children and are deciding what values to impart to them. And the youngest are going through the formative years of late adolescence and early adulthood. As we shall see we need to identify when is the best time to transmit faith and how to do it appropriately at that time.

A third element to keep in mind as think of generation is the socializing role of the age cohort. Schulze's research, the results of which will be explored later, indicates that the two most important factors in the shaping of worldview and mores are age and education.

---

6. See especially Wade Clark Roof, A Generation of Seekers: The Spiritual Journey of the Baby Boom Generation (San Francisco: Harper, 1993) and the literature cited, 269ff.
7. On the latter, less studied group, see William Strauss and Neil Howell, Generations: The History of America's Future (New York: Morrow, 1992).
8. Roof, op.cit., ch. 9.

His comment about age points to similar findings elsewhere about to what extent we are socialized now into our society by our age peers and not by the older generation. This is caused partially by parents' spending less time with their children because of work obligations, and also partially by mass media that aim programming at particular age groups. Living also in a culture where old means out-of-date and obsolete, people in these age cohorts are less likely to look to their elders for guidance. And also, the baby boomers are a big enough cohort not to need to turn to others. The popular American television show 'thirtysomething' was indicative of this. For the cohort behind the baby boomers, to trust elders is to trust the boomers who have (sometimes as parents) messed up their lives.

What this socializing role of the cohort means is that, more than ever, we need to work within these cohorts to transmit the Christian faith and not simply between them. These two important cohorts are more likely to look to their own rather than to others for guidance.

3. When to Transmit the Faith

In the past, it has been believed that the transmittal of Christian faith should begin at the same time as the transmittal of other values. That continues to be a valid concept. Wade Clark Roof's research on the baby boom generation indicated that childhood religious education was an important factor in many of the boomers' decision to return to institutional religion, both in their own memory and in their desire for their children to have a similar upbringing. On the other hand, at least for some, memories of what had been imparted helped confirm the decision not to return to religious practice.[9] The results, therefore, are mixed. If religious education is not continued after childhood, Christian faith can be seen as something for children or something to keep us childish. It appears likely in most any event to be rebelled against in adolescence.

Late adolescence and early adulthood constitute the second period upon which to reflect. This is a period of 'conversion' for many, and is the period when young people are likely to experiment with a variety of religious possibilities, including what are sometimes called cults. It is a period of opening to faith, but one that is conditioned by many other things – especially whatever form of faith had been transmitted by parents.

The faith of those in middle age is an area not concentrated upon sufficiently. Those seeking an integrated balance in their lives may turn back to the beliefs of their youth, or find themselves seeking out more appropriate

9.   Roof, op.cit., ch. 6.

approaches to their stage in life. This is an area for the transmittal of faith often overlooked because it is deemed as 'too late.' But some research does point to the older edge of the baby boom cohort becoming more reflective and hungry for something larger than themselves. The sheer size of the cohort calls itself to our attention.

So what can be said about when to transmit the Christian faith? One is best perhaps pragmatic about this: whenever the opportunity presents itself. The 'how' of transmittal also has to be attended to. Childhood transmittal should, of course, be done from a child's point of view. Most important it would seem would be to teach the great stories that embody what it means to be a Christian, both the biblical stories and those of the heroic men and women of Christian history. Adolescent teaching might best focus on Jesus the teacher, to speak of the values that help configure a Christian life. Middle adult teaching would stress the wisdom and mystical elements. I am not an expert in religious education, and these agenda might be filled out better by them than by me. But these would seem to be points of departure adequate to the age.

4. What is Mediated?

The last reflections on when to transmit Christian faith moved necessarily into the 'what' of faith. Catechisms served this purpose in both Catholic and Reformation Christianity since the beginning of modernity. The two cohorts we have been concentrating upon were raised with television, which means that they appear to be more visual than verbal. Moreover, they have elaborate expectations about entertainment, and inasmuch as religion fits into the leisure (i.e., non-work) time, it participates in the entertainment expectation, whether we deem that theologically admissible or not. Rather than dismissing this as an unacceptable point of departure, we need to ask ourselves: just what is it we want to transmit in the transmittal of faith?

To begin with lists of doctrines would likely be a move in the wrong direction. Given some of the features we will look at in the next two sections of this paper, one might begin by looking at imparting a Christian identity. That would involve teachings, but teachings embedded in a community which continues to shape its life by the great Christian narratives.[10] These need

---

10. This approach is suggested strongly in Robert Wuthnow, Christianity in the Twenty-First Century: Reflections on the Challenge Ahead (New York: Oxford University Press, 1993).

to be what Robert Bellah has called 'communities of memory'[11] rather than lifestyle enclaves of the like-minded sharing a similar lifestyle. Those narratives of faith not only define our memory; they shape our experience of the present. The configuration or emphases in the narratives change over time, and change as they engage our present experience. If our doctrines are to make sense, they must find location within those narratives as those narratives engage and help explain the present. Examples of this will follow in the next two sections.

5. The Risk Society and the Transmittal of Faith

The publication in 1986 of Ulrich Beck's 'Risikogesellschaft: Auf dem Weg in eine andere Moderne' has contributed significantly to our understanding of the shape of our current society – call it post-modern, post-industrial or whatever. Beck speaks of a reflexive modernity, that is, a modernity that is able to turn back on itself and relativize itself in some measure. Where modern societies now are is a matter of some debate. While there is much of the modernist agenda that most would not want to abandon (such as human rights or individual freedom), the limits of modernity's claims for itself are now being keenly felt. The securing of social boundaries by the nation-state and the protection of the individual in his or her own freedom cast shadows as well. The nation-state, once the vehicle of change and growth, can now become an obstacle to it. Individual freedom can lead to isolation and alienation.

Beck tries to describe the society we are now in beyond the industrial society and the economic metaphors that encoded its messages. He calls this new society the risk society, as the risks that threaten survival are redistributed in a totalizing, scientized, global society. Those threats are the most obvious in the ecological sphere, but also evident in pharmaceutics, and the redistribution of work and gender roles.

There are many themes that could be explored regarding the risk society, but for our purposes here I wish to concentrate on two, both related to what Beck calls the scientization of knowledge. These are: a sense of contingency and the release of alternative rationalities.

Beck explores in his book what he calls the 'politics of knowledge,' i.e., what will count for true knowledge in society and who will determine such. Beck sees that in the Enlightenment a 'primary scientization' of knowledge took place, where the new scientific approach pitted itself against the

---

11. Robert Bellah et al., Habits of the Heart (Berkeley: University of California Press, 1985). The term was first used by the American philosopher Josiah Royce.

established forms of knowledge, religion and tradition, and the authorities (mainly ecclesiastical) that maintained them. This strategy called for a scientization of knowledge that all true knowledge would have to be scientific to be deemed true. This represented the first, or primary stage of scientization.

Through the nineteenth century and into the early twentieth there was a confidence that science would ultimately displace religion and tradition as valid forms of knowledge. During this time religion and tradition found themselves to be on the defensive, alternately denying that religion had anything to do with science, or affirming that the two were not contradictory. The battles were fought largely on science's terms, however.

The primary scientization of knowledge has succeeded in convincing most moderns that it is the supreme form of knowledge. But what has happened in the meantime is that the scientific circle has not been closed. Not only is not everything explained, but more importantly, science has come up against its own fallibility. In attempts to improve the world, it has succeeded also in making it a worse place. And like the sorcerer's apprentice, it has unleashed new dangers (especially of a petrochemical or pharmaceutical nature) into the world. The knowledge of these new risks, which point directly at the fallibility of science, is knowledge that must be controlled and kept from circulation in society. This leads to a second stage of scientization, 'reflexive scientization,'' where science is not pitted against religion and tradition, but is used to obscure or cover up its own mistakes.[12]

This prompts reflection on two things pertinent to our discussions here. First of all, on contingency. In the totalizing nature of a scientized discourse, supported in turn by a global capitalism and a global hyperculture, contingency is supposed to disappear. But as in every other utopian dream to date, contingency continues to intrude on the politically managed reality. To effect complete control, contingency must be eliminated and, failing that, discourse about contingency must be suppressed. Beck sees this option being followed in the risk society. The general public is not allowed to question scientific mistakes and is instead urged to believe in science more so that they will go away.

Christian theology needs to reassert itself regarding risk and contingency in reflexive modern society. People experience contingency but either do not know how to identify it or try to drown out its voice in an entertainment level of society (to use Schulze's categorization).[13] Contingency is part of human existence, and not facing up to it does harm to our humanity.

---

12. Beck, op.cit., ch.2.
13. Schulze, op.cit., section 6.6.

Along with the exposure of the great strength but less than total infallibility, reflexive modernity opens the door to alternative rationalities. It means overcoming the idea that there is but one rationality, and it belongs to science. It means also not acquiescing in the narratives of this scientific rationality and being willing to set forth other accounts of the world in which we live. In postmodern readings of our society, room is at least being made for alternative narratives and their rationalities, even if few such narratives are emerging. The most persuasive new narratives in our society have been, to my mind, of feminist construction. Liberation narratives have also changed the way many of us think.

Because a narrative has cohesion and can articulate its rationality does not, of course, make it true. Our century has already witnessed too much of this totalitarian form of narrative to be lulled into believing this. Narratives and rationalities still need to prove themselves in communities and between communities. But what it does do or should do is to embolden Christians to put forward from the many strands of their Great Tradition plausible narratives that both engage the world and critique it at the same time. The success of the Reformation was largely one of the creating of such narratives, focusing on the alienation and anxieties of the emerging modern individual, and assuring and 'giving comfort' (to use the words of the Heidelberg Catechism) in God's justifying grace to the struggling, anxious soul of early modernity. It was a narrative that focused on the individual. It was, at least in Reformed theology, cast in the larger language of the day (of Hobbes and Grotius) of the unmediated individual, contract, property and law.[14]

The Reformation took hold in northern Europe, because it embodied the conditions and the possibilities to deal both with the emerging modern individual and the new capitalism. We need such boldness again today in retelling the Christian story. I will make some suggestions about this in the next section. What is important to emphasize here is that theology should take a less defensive stance against secularization and develop its own rationalities. It needs to address from a contextual perspective why these local theologies came to be translocal. And from this recovery of traditions see how those traditions can form patterns for community in the postmodern situation. There have always been multiple rationalities, sometimes overt, sometimes hidden. Feminists and other cultural historians have been uncovering these. The multicultural reality of our societies urges us to do the same. And the communalists (to use a broad category to cover a wide range of philosophers and political scientists) seem already to be pointing in that direction. To see

---

14. For a study of the philosophical forces at work here, see John Milbank, Theology and Social Theory (Oxford: Basil Blackwell, 1991), 9-48.

Christian tradition as traditions – as local theologies – that represent a reconfiguration of the biblical narrative in light of changing cultural circumstances is to retrieve the tradition not as one totalizing form of discourse over against another, but as persuasive alternatives.

6. The Experience Society

The discussion of elements in the understanding of the risk society was directed principally to those who bear responsibility for transmitting Christian faith, urging them to reconfigure Christian narrative in light of postmodern reality and in the space that postmodernity provides for it. We turn now to a closer look at the receivers of this narrative.

This group has been characterized for us masterfully by Gerhard Schulze in his 'Die Erlebnisgesellschaft: Zur Kultursoziologie der Gegenwart'. This study of German society at the beginning of the 1990's is incomplete (it admittedly does not consider non-German ethnic groups or East Germans), but nonetheless does provide an important picture of how a Northern European society is changing.

Schulze's central argument is that a society that has created wealth and material abundance reaches a certain threshold that fundamentally results in a reordering of that society. The 'experience society' of the title is the new society that Germany is becoming. What happens as scarcity and the struggle to survive are decentered from the place they occupy in most societies is that a new ordering of society emerges. The economic metaphors that are used to characterize an industrial society are replaced by what Schulze calls a psychophysical semantics that turn the focus away from the means of production to the individual self. As the workworld recedes in importance, more energies are directed to the lifeworld and the construction of the self. Overcoming scarcity is replaced by making choices. Similarly, a class structure in society, largely the product of how groups related to the means of industrial production, is replaced by other forms of segmentation related to the construction of the self. Out of his data, Schulze constructs five segmentations or milieux: niveau milieu, integrative milieu, selfrealization milieu, harmony milieu, and entertainment milieu. As was noted above, Schulze also discovered that age and education were key factors in restructuring society. For the purposes of looking at the two age cohorts discussed above – those born between 1946 and 1964 (boomers), and those born between 1965 and 1979 (post-boomers), we will concentrate on the two milieus where most of them cluster: the self-realization milieu and the entertainment milieu. The self-realization group enjoys a higher level of education (in the German system, "mittlere Reife und berufsbildende Schule to Abitur und Universtät"), while the entertainment group represents the lower strata of secondary education ("mittlere Reife und Lehre down to Hauptschule ohne Lehre or ohne Abschluss"). The self-realization milieu seeks out choices for constructing the self that are upscale in nature (boutiques, newer cafés, jogging, bicycling). They see themselves as active in a wide variety of activities that both express and enhance their self-definition. They seek their stimulation in trying different things and exotic holidays. While active, they are given also to contemplation, monitoring whether their activities and the pleasures they provide are enhancing their sense of self-realization.

While somewhat given to narcissism, they do reach out to others and seek a certain perfection. They are diffusely religious and non-institutional.

Those predominantly in the entertainment milieu are in the same age group as the self-realizers, but with less education. They are high on action, as are the self-realizers, but do not show the same propensity to contemplation. They prefer mass sporting events like football or pinball arcades. While the self-realizers are more likely to read 'Der Spiegel' and 'Die Zeit', and watch documentaries and commentary programs on television, those in the entertainment milieu read 'Bildzeitung' and the local newspaper, and watch videos and American detective programs on television. In place of contemplative moments to enhance the self, those in the entertainment milieu are more likely to fill up the void with more action, either to divert themselves (entertainment) or to enhance their identification with their chosen lifestyle. They tend to have little interest in religion.

Both groups can be easily stereotyped as materialists or consumerists, as they often are in church pronouncements. But to write them off is to miss the point of this conference: how is Christian faith transmitted in this kind of culture, which may be the only kind of culture we have at this time?

This is a culture marked by prosperity, where for the first time large numbers of people may participate. The kind of culture that emerges in the experience society may seem unprincipled and trivial, and it can undoubtedly become so. Both of the milieus described can be moderately anti-institutional because they trust that the institutions will always be there, guaranteeing them the necessary employment to secure a salary or wage. And so, if all systems stay in place, participants in both milieux will continue to prosper.

Can the Christian narrative be so configured as to engage this culture from within and bring about both its elevation and its transformation? It would seem to me that there are some possibilities worth exploring. We must be aware, however, that choice plays a large role in the thinking of this group. They prefer the bricolage of a life-style put together out of specialty shops (self-realizers) or mass discount shopping malls (entertainment). And their approach to something like the Christian tradition will seem, at least at first, too eclectic or selective. But should not their selectivity be taken just as seriously (and then as critically) as that of previous generations of Christians?

Could making the Letter to the Romans the center of the Gospel message not be considered overly selective? Or the christologies of John and Paul as preferred over those of the Synoptics? Or our imposing of sixteenth and seventeenth century ecclesiologies on Africa, Latin America and Asia rather arbitrary? Let us give these contemporary groups a chance.

I would suggest that, at least for the self-realizers, the wisdom traditions of Christianity be emphasized in retelling the Christian story. That would include the submerged Sophia traditions that feminist scholarship has retrieved, as well as the Gnostic and mystical spiritual traditions of Christianity. On that basis there can be yet another rereading of the story of Jesus to parallel the intense readings now going on elsewhere around the world. These represent an attempt to find in the story of Jesus those elements that engage the culture more directly and thereby creation of the conditions of possibility for critique. Wisdom can be taken up selectively, but ultimately it too is threaded together into a tradition.

The findings in Roof's study of American baby boomers would seem to support this proposal. Jesus was attractive to those whom Roof studied not as divine nor as a Savior, but because of his teaching and his moral example. It is Jesus' teaching and his example that make him attractive to these cohorts of choosers.

Another thing should be noted. While tradition is not an intelligible category to most of these people, community is. And tradition will only become plausible if it is enacted in a credible community. These people are not afraid of discipline (after all, they frequent athletic facilities regularly!), but they are suspicious of authority imposed for no credible reason. Grounding tradition in credible communities may be the most important condition for our transmitting the faith. Among the younger edge of these cohorts, finding a plausible way to make choices attracts them to places where the Gospel is really lived. To some of us older than they the form may look too authoritarian, but it should only tell us that they are looking for coherent ways to structure their choices. On the older edge of these cohorts, now into middle age, the quest for wisdom becomes paramount in importance. The balancing of life in a questing community is their aim.

7. Conclusion

In the course of this presentation I have tried to focus us on what will be involved in the transgenerational mediation of faith, as to whom, when, how and what we do. This was followed by the investigation into two recent sociological descriptions of a European society to see what, they could raise up for us as considerations for our task. Looking at Beck's risk society suggested a way of retrieving our traditions in a pluralist society with multiple rationalities. Schulze's experience society suggested just which of those traditions might be most useful in transmitting the faith to the generations that, at least in terms of their stages of life, might be most ready for it. The suggestion that we explore our wisdom traditions, both to provide moral guidance and spiritual refinement, is intended to point us toward the first steps we might take to engage the experience society. Finally, it was emphasized again that this transmittal cannot simply be the passing on of doctrine. It must be enacted in plausible communities that draw their lives from this tradition.

Transmitting faith is a formidable task for every generation. Ours has its special complications, some of which were only referred to here. Some of them, like the multicultural reality, need more work regarding how communities are formed under these circumstances before one can speak of how to transmit faith within them. But forge ahead we must, using our best lights and with trust that God will be with us. I close with the suggestion that the Emmaus story of Luke 24 may be our best guide in this: listen quietly for a long time, and then open the Scriptures in such a way that hearts might be on fire. Heavy-handed authority will not produce results. But the whisperings of the Spirit will.

III Models of Revelation in the Context of the Enlightenment:

Empirical Research into the Content Dimension of Religious Socialisation

Chris A.M. Hermans

Research into the content of religious socialisation often focuses on certain doctrines or religious practices. In this contribution we will ask a more fundamental question: What do religious people understand by faith?

In Christianity the conception of faith is related to the conception of revelation. Revelation can for example refer to the deposit of faith, which one must believe without being able to understand. However, revelation can also refer to the process in which God reveals himself in the personal encounter between people. It makes quite a difference for religious socialisation which conception one takes as a starting-point. In the first case handing down propositions of faith is central. In the second case the central issue is the clarification of human experience from a religious perspective. In this contribution we will consider which models of revelation are present in the religious consciousness of modern man. Various models are handed down by all kinds of institutions (the Church, parents, school). But to what purpose? To what extent are these models also present as conceptions in people's consciousness? Who are typical representatives of a certain conception of faith?

These questions are related to the opposition between revelation and the Enlightenment. The Enlightenment started a process of modernisation which focuses exclusively on the autonomous subject who wants to take a stand or make a choice on the basis of his own insights. Is this not diametrically opposed to Christian revelation? Do some models agree more with our modern feeling for life than others?

1. Religious Socialisation

Religious socialisation refers to the handing down of Christianity in the broadest sense of the word (Kaufman & Stachel 1980, p. 135). It is characteristically unplanned, i.e. it serves no explicit educational purpose.

Religious socialisation has a content and a social dimension. The social dimension relates to the structural and institutional conditions in which man develops his identity as a Christian. The content dimension refers to the content of the Christian identity as it finds expression in its different aspects: propositions of faith, religious practices (rituals, devotional practices), religious experiences, religious knowledge (of rituals, traditions, the Bible etc.) and the implications of religious commitment for daily life (Stark & Glock 1968, pp. 14-16).

The crisis in which religious socialisation finds itself in our society concerns both its content and its social dimension. The process of modernisation, which has taken place in our society since the Enlightenment, helps us to understand the nature of this crisis.

Modernisation has radically changed the social conditions for religious socialisation (Kaufman & Stachel 1980, pp. 125-126). In pre-modern society man's identity was determined by an all-encompassing symbolic universe shared by all and largely dominated by Christianity. The exclusive basis for social cohesion between individuals was the local community, in which individuals were fully integrated. This integration was based on common mores, which in western society were to a great extent dictated by Christian institutions (such as the rhythm of the Christian year). This implied that a child grew up within a local community whose mores and social ties (including the Church) were taken for granted. In modern society the all-encompassing symbolic universe has made way for different sectors, each of which has its own conceptual framework and criteria. In each of these sectors people play certain roles: employee, consumer, pupil, church member etc. A shared identity is based on a common functional role and not necessarily on a common set of mores. Identification with a social group is always partial, never complete. In these conditions developing a religious identity as a Christian has become much more problematic. The presence of Christian tradition in society is mainly limited to the Church as an institution, which is only one of a number of sectors. At the same time one's identity as a Christian is only part of one's identity and not necessarily a central or integral part. People belong to very heterogeneous groups, each of which they only partially identify with. Where do generations growing up in this situation find socialising institutions to hand down faith? Is it true that the domestic environment is the only institution in this situation that can influence the development of the Christian identity of future generations? (Van der Slik 1992).

Also the content of religious socialisation has become problematic as a result of the process of modernisation. Here we are not so much concerned with the fact that certain religious beliefs or rituals have lost their plausibility. The problem is a more fundamental one: the credibility of faith as such is at stake. Does faith not clash with modern times, which are characterised by the process of rationalisation? By rationalisation we mean the process of making our thinking and actions manageable (Habermas 1981; Schreuder 1985). Truth is no longer determined by some external authority, but by arguments. This does not mean that rationality is synonymous with the instrumental rationality of economics and technology. Each sector of society has its own rationality to the extent that there are characteristic arguments and criteria underlying certain actions. Scientists, for example, try to formulate laws of nature on the basis of experiments. In the bureaucratic machinery of the state (e.g. health care) the central aim is the efficient and effective application of rules and regulations. In the administration of justice the correct application of the laws and jurisprudence is central. In the field of religion, however, this process of rationalisation raises serious questions. Are faith and intellect not diametrically opposed? Is it possible to give arguments that provide an insight into faith? Does faith not ultimately rely on the authority of revelation?

2. The Enlightenment and Revelation

Revelation is a self-evident concept in present-day theology. It has become synonymous with the content of Christian faith. This shows from statements like: 'Revelation teaches us...' or 'In the context of revelation it is clear that...' (Eicher 1977, p. 49). A theological exposition of faith and experience begins with a reflection on revelation both as every-day experience and as an element of Christian religious tradition (e.g. Schillebeeckx 1980, p. 76ff.). However, revelation has only been given this central position since the 18th and 19th centuries as a result of the confrontation with the Enlightenment. In the Enlightenment Christianity was called to account to prove its claim on truth. In this process the concept of revelation played a central part.

Revelation served to annihilate the criticism directed against the Christian claim on truth by the Enlightenment. This annihilation was made possible by the introduction of a specific concept of revelation with the following characteristics (Seckler 1980, p. 33):
– Revelation has a supernaturalistic character, i.e. revelation is considered to be distinct from human nature and therefore inaccessible to reason. Revelation can only be accepted in an act of surrender.

– The second characteristic is a revelational positivism in which the fact that revelation is handed down is equalled with its truth. The mere fact that the propositions of faith have been handed down by tradition and doctrinal authority is taken as a sufficient basis for their acceptance.

– Revelation has an absolutist character in that its truth derives from an incomprehensible exercise of God's will demanding man's unquestioning submission. The truth of revelation can only be founded on extrinsic or external circumstances (*criteria externa revelationis*) such as the miracles of Jesus or his resurrection.

Such a conception of revelation may successfully annihilate the rational criticism directed against Christian faith, but at the same time it places Christianity outside modern culture. Such a strategy can only be used to oppose modern times, which is exactly what the Church and Christian theology did (Seckler 1980, p. 54ff.; Eicher 1977, p. 53ff.). Revelation served as a battle cry in the fight against the Enlightenment and rational attempts to give meaning to life. This opposition by Roman-Catholic doctrinal authority and orthodox theologians lasted until the second Vatican Council. This does not mean that there were no movements among Catholic theologians that sought a dialogue with modern thinking, for example 'modernism' (among others Loisy, Tyrell, von Hügel) and the 'nouvelle théologie' (among others Chenu, de Lubac). The break-through in the Catholic Church, however, came with the dogmatic constitution on divine revelation (Dei Verbum) in the second Vatican Council. In this constitution the idea that God reveals certain supernatural secrets is no longer central, but God is seen as primarily revealing himself. God discloses himself to man as the reality that liberates humankind. In the 19th and 20th centuries Protestant theologians developed several alternatives to the strategy of annihilation. Some of these alternatives will be discussed below.

3. Models of Revelation

In present-day theology several models of revelation can be found. By a model we mean a root metaphor with a lasting force and sufficient stability to give a comprehensive and coherent explanation of a certain object, fact or event (McFague 1987). A model contains the central inspiration for a certain conception of revelation, such as 'revelation as doctrine' (Vaticanum I). This means that the content of the concept of revelation is determined by doctrine. In this context revelation consists of the deposit of faith demanding acceptance on the part of the believer.

Several classifications of models of revelations are found in theology. The best-known are those of the German theologian Eicher (1976; 1977) and the English theologian Dulles (1983). Unlike Eicher, Dulles offers a typology of models consisting of the following models:

A revelation as doctrine
B revelation as history
C revelation as inner experience
D revelation as dialectical presence
E revelation as new awareness

According to Dulles, this typology contains the most important of the current models of revelation (Dulles 1983, p. 28). We will adopt his typology with two amendments. First, Dulles says that he finds it difficult to place the thinking of liberation theology, because it is in a state of flux. He has now situated it in the model of revelation as 'new awareness', but suggests that it may develop into an independent model. We will not regard liberation theology as a separate model, either. However, we do think that its place in the fifth model of revelation is curious. It seems more correct to situate liberation theology in the second model of 'revelation as history', as Eicher does (Eicher 1976, p. 121ff.). Secondly, we will add a sixth model to Dulles' typology, which is also found with Eicher (1976, p. 126ff.): the model of the interpersonal encounter.

Below we will give a short description of the types. This description is largely based on Dulles (1983). At the end of each description some statements will be given which are characteristic of a certain type. These statements will be formulated in terms of faith (for example, 'Faith refers to the deposit of divinely revealed truth.').

Revelation can refer to different things (Eicher 1977, pp. 22-48).
– First, revelation can be used as a metaphor for the foundation of religion. As a metaphor it refers to the transcendental basis of religion which can never be unambiguously expressed in conceptual formulations. We are dealing with a mystery that can merely be hinted at by words.
– Secondly, revelation can be regarded as a category of a specific type of religious experience. It refers to experiences in which the transcendental basis of religion reveals itself to man.
– Thirdly, revelation can be seen as a category of theological reflection. As a theological category revelation serves to provide the theological system with internal coherence: from the interpretation of Scripture to the unity of the

Church.

By formulating the statements in terms of faith we will take as our starting-point the second interpretation of revelation as based on experience. We will do so with a view to the empirical-theological research in which these statements will be used.

A Revelation as Doctrine

'According to this view revelation is principally found in clear propositional statements attributed to God as authoritative teacher. For Protestants who accept this approach, revelation is generally identified with the Bible, viewed as a collection of inspired and inerrant teachings. For Catholic representatives of this approach, revelation is to be found, at least most accessibly, in the official teaching of the Church, viewed as infallible oracle' (Dulles 1983, p. 27). This conception was dominant in Catholic neo-Scholastic theology from 1850 till about 1950. The conciliar and Roman documents of this period gave official support to this model as may be seen from the Constitution on Catholic Faith issued by the first Vatican Council (1870). Revelation is seen as a supernatural doctrine which is inaccessible or at least barely accessible to reason. The virtue of faith lies in obediently accepting the truth of the incomprehensible 'veritas revelatae' (Seckler 1985, p. 65ff.) 'The ecclesiastical teaching office (or 'magisterium') is the proximate and universal norm for determining what is revelation. When the universal magisterium (consisting of the pope and the bishops who teach in unison with him) teaches something as a dogma, its teaching is infallible, since Christ has promised not to desert his followers in their exercise of their ministry. One must therefore believe the dogmas as though they were uttered by Christ himself. In equating the dogmas of the Church with divine revelation the neo-Scholastics are faithful to their propositional understanding of revelation. The concept of dogma as a divinely revealed truth serves in turn to reinforce the propositional view of revelation' (Dulles 1983, p. 44). The authority of reve-aled truths can be 'proved' by certain signs. Particularly miracles and prophesies are powerful signs of the truth of revelation. In this context the resurrection of Jesus is seen as the greatest of all miracles.

Statements
A1 Faith refers to the deposit of divinely revealed truth.
A2 Faith refers to the deposit of truth which directs our lives to God.
A3 Faith is the acceptance of inexplicable propositional truths founded on the reality of God.

A4 The truth of faith is proved by the miracles in the Bible.

A5 The truth of faith is guaranteed by the interpretation of Scripture by the Church.

B Revelation as History

'This type of theory, proposed in conscious opposition to the preceding, maintains that God reveals himself primarily in his great deeds, especially those which form the major themes of biblical history. The Bible and the official teaching of the Church are considered to embody revelation only to the extent that they are reliable reports about what God has done. Although some adherents of this approach look upon biblical and ecclesiastical teaching as revelation in a derivative sense, most prefer to say that the Bible and Church teaching are rather *witnesses* to revelation' (Dulles 1983, p. 27). This model of revelation became very popular among theologians as a result of the works of Oscar Cullman in the forties. God's plan reveals itself in history (Eicher 1976, p. 119ff.). The Bible can be seen as revelation not because it accurately recounts history from a human point of view but because it narrates and interprets the actions of God in history.

The weakness of this approach is that Christian tradition is reduced to its historic origin in Jesus of Nazareth. It leaves little room for the critical power of the belief in Christ (Eicher 1976, p. 120). Two other theological approaches that also belong to the model of revelation as history do have this critical power. They both consider history from the point of view of its fulfilment at some point in the future.

First of all there is the approach of Wolfgang Pannenberg's theology of universal history. The Kingdom of God reverses the usual relationship between present and future in seeing the future as an extension of the present (Pannenberg 1971). It is not the present which is decisive for the future but the future which determines the meaning of the present. God's promise means that the future is not a black hole. People may live their lives in the confidence that God will make history turn out right. This ultimate meaning of history already became visible in the death and resurrection of Jesus Christ (Eicher 1977, p. 430ff.).

Also in liberation theology the present is subject to the promise of fulfilment in the future (Gutierrez 1974). The Kingdom of God refers to the wholeness which God will realise in the future. This is guaranteed by God himself. Therefore it is beyond any doubt. This certainty inspires an unconditional dedication to this coming Kingdom of God in people. This involves paying special attention to the poor and oppressed. Anything we do for these humble ones, we do for Jesus (Matt. 25:45).

The first three of the following statements refer to Pannenberg's theology of universal history; the last three refer to the approach of liberation theology.

Statements
B1 In the Bible God reveals himself as the ultimate goal of history.
B2 Faith is man's response to the nature of history as leading to an ultimate goal.
B3 Faith answers the question about the meaning of life from the point of view of the future fulfilment by God.
B4 Faith is man's liberating dedication to the poor in the context of the coming Kingdom of God.
B5 Faith is the liberation of the poor and oppressed in the light of the fulfilment of history by God.
B6 Faith is man's dedication to the poor and oppressed based on the certainty of the future fulfilment of the world by God.

C Revelation as Inner Experience

In this model revelation takes the form of an immediate interior experience. 'For most authors this consists in a direct, unmediated encounter with the divine, although some affirm, with the biblical and Christian tradition, that this experience is to be found in communion with the prophets and especially with Jesus, whose familiarity with God was unsurpassably intimate. Thus faith possesses a kind of 'mediated immediacy' ... The content of this model is God as he lovingly communicates himself to the soul that is open to him' (Dulles 1983, pp. 76-77).

According to Dulles, various theologians belong to this model, like H. Wheeler Robinson, C.H. Dodd, John Hick and some Catholic modernists like Tyrell. Emphasising the element of immediacy, these theologians generally deny that there are such things as revealed doctrines. They draw a sharp distinction between faith, as the acceptance of revelation, and belief, as the subscription to doctrine. In this sense also Bultmann fits into this model, although Dulles situates him in the dialectical model (see D below). This shows from the following quotation of Bultmann which we find with Dulles: 'The truth does not exist as a doctrine... Rather the position a man takes vis-à-vis the Revealer decides not whether he knows the truth, but whether he is 'of the truth'' (Dulles 1983, p. 88). In his encounter with God man gets to know himself better than he could have done by himself. Man's inner experience of faith provides them with a new, deeper insight into himself.

Statements
C1 Faith is man's direct experience of God's closeness.
C2 Faith originates in man's encounter with God in Scripture.
C3 The Bible appeals to man to decide whether or not to believe that God is close to man.
C4 Faith is man's decision to give a new meaning to human existence.
C5 Faith is an event providing man with a new insight into himself.

D Revelation as Dialectical Presence

'A number of European theologians, especially in the years following World War I, repudiated both the objectivism of the first two types of revelation theology and the subjectivism of the third. God, they insisted, could never be an object known either by inference from nature or history, by propositional teaching, or by direct perception of a mystical kind. Utterly transcendent, God encounters the human subject when it pleases him by means of a word in which faith recognizes him to be present. The word of God simultaneously reveals and conceals the divine presence' (Dulles 1983, p. 28). The most famous proponent of this model is undoubtedly Karl Barth. According to Barth, God has unsurpassably revealed himself to man in Jesus Christ. We do not encounter God, but we know God because he has encountered us through Christ. Whatever is regarded as revelation beyond this is a human illusion; it is even sinful (Eicher 1977, p. 251).

Statements
D1 We can only know God through Jesus.
D2 Faith has only been made possible by man's redemption by Jesus Christ.
D3 Faith is only possible thanks to the biblical account of God's word.
D4 To believe that we can know God by reason is a human illusion.
D5 The mind of a sinful man is blind to God's truth.

E Revelation as New Awareness

What characterises this model is that revelation is not seen as something given from outside, descending from above upon the human subject. Faith is not a new knowledge added to human knowledge, but a new consciousness created by the Christian message (Dulles 1983, p. 106ff.). The whole of human history is regarded as being under the influence of God's grace. Grace is universally offered to mankind. But if grace is universal, so is revelation. Christian faith is the explication and specification of this mystery that takes place everywhere. Faith is founded on the human self, in which a longing for definitiveness and infinity is present. Faith is a transcendental possibility. In Jesus Christ all that man truly hopes and longs for has unsurpassably taken shape. This has provided human hope for infinity with a firm foundation (Rahner 1976, p. 264ff.). But God is not an exclusive possession of Christians. A God who has involved himself in a partnership with all of humanity is revealed wherever there are people.

The consciousness or awareness model has its philosophical ancestry in the transcendental idealism of Kant and the subjective idealism of Fichte. It has come to Catholic theology partly through the influence of Maurice Blondel. Karl Rahner is perhaps the most famous proponent of this model.

Statements
E1 Faith is man's natural orientation towards an ultimate goal.
E2 Faith is essential for man as a longing for an ultimate meaning of life.
E3 Faith is essential for man as a longing for infinity.
E4 Faith is man's longing for a definitive answer to the incomprehensibility of human existence.
E5 Faith is man's true openness to a definitive answer to human questions.

F Revelation as Interpersonal Encounter

Characteristic of this model is the fact that it no longer focuses on the self as a questioning creature but takes the personal unity of the We as its starting-point (Eicher 1976, p. 126). This model has been greatly influenced by Jewish thinkers like Martin Buber and Emmanuel Levinas. It is not the Cartesian subject that is central, but the category of the encounter or dialogue. In the encounter we are not so much concerned with two subjects and the relationship they enter into. Central in the 'dia-logue' is the category of the 'between' ('dia') (Levinas 1981). It is in the 'between' of the encounter that people become I and You. This interpersonal space of the encounter transcends the I and You. In the 'between' people are approached by a Thou (God) who appeals to us. Levinas has given a highly ethical interpretation to this appeal. In the countenance of the other person we see a reflection of the Other Person (God). This other person appeals to us to take our responsibility as human beings. Only by answering this appeal does man become his true self, i.e. a responsible human being.

Statements
F1 Faith is the experience of God in the countenance of one's fellow man.
F2 Man experiences God in deeply human encounters.
F3 Faith is the experience of God in the deep love between people.
F4 In our genuine encounters with other people God shows himself as a person who appeals to us.
F5 Faith is the process of becoming truly human in genuine encounters with other people.

4. Research

4.1 Research Questions

Religious socialisation is the implicit process by which people develop their identity as Christians. The different models of revelation that were discussed above are all found in present-day Christianity, at least on a theological level. The question we are concerned with here is whether they are also present as conceptions in the religious consciousness of Christians. This religious consciousness gives us an insight into the outcome of the process of religious socialisation to which people have been subjected.

In our research we have been guided by the following questions:
1) Which models of revelation are present in the religious consciousness of core members of the Catholic church?
2) How strong is the preference for these models?
3) Is there a relation between these models in the religious consciousness of core members of the Catholic church?
4) Who are the typical representatives of the different models of revelation?
5) Is the preference for a specific model influenced by a heteronomous or autonomous attitude towards religion?

We will comment briefly on the last question. This question is crucial for the concept of revelation in modern society. All the above-mentioned models try to cope with the problem of revelation in the context of the Enlightenment. Each model offers a different solution to this problem. The question we will consider here is how successful these models are in modern culture, in which the autonomous subject refuses to accept ideas on the basis of authority. Does a heteronomous or autonomous attitude of people influence their preference for a specific model of revelation? Are some models more in harmony with the modern mind than others?

What answers may we expect to these questions? According to Dulles, the first four models (A-D) have in common a view of revelation as coming from outside (Dulles 1983, p. 98). 'The recipient of revelation is viewed as passive. The content of revelation is regarded as being beyond the reach of human experience and human heuristic powers' (ibid.). The fifth model abandons this concept, assigning the human subject an active role in the process of revelation. 'By situating revelation within the individual psyche, in its socio-cultural context, this model escapes an unwelcome authoritarianism and appeals to minds enamoured of freedom and progress' (Dulles 1983, pp. 110-111).

Also Eicher states that the models of revelation as doctrine (A) and revelation as dialectical presence (C) are formulated in opposition to the Enlightenment (Eicher 1977, p. 63). In his view not only the model of new awareness (E) but also the model of history (B), for example in the person of Wolfgang Pannenberg, abandons the heteronomous point of view. They preserve modern self-awareness, at the same time transforming it from a Christian perspective.

4.2 Research Population and Method
The research population consists of adult core members of the Catholic church. Core members are people who regularly go to church (at least once a month) and who are active as a volunteers within their parish (for example as members of a choir or as volunteers helping young children to prepare for their first Communion). We may expect these core members to have a relatively well-developed identity as Christians. If a model of revelation is present in the process of religious socialisation of Catholic people, it should be possible to assess its presence in the religious consciousness of these core members.

In our research we focused on core members who were following a two-year pastoral course. These courses are organised by pastoral centres in every diocese in the Netherlands. In the first half of 1990 we sent 547 questionnaires to people following a pastoral course. A total of 350 questionnaires were returned and could be used in the analysis.

We will give a short impression of the research population. Seven out of ten respondents are women. The average age is 43. Nearly all respondents feel a strong commitment to their parish (four out of five). The majority have lived in their parish for more than ten years. People from smaller towns and villages are overrepresented in the research population: 37% live in a town or village smaller than 10,000 inhabitants. Only 14% live in a city larger than 100,000 inhabitants. Finally, there are many highly-educated people in the research population: 34% have completed some form of higher education.

4.3 Research Results

1) Which models of revelation are present in the religious consciousness of core members of the Catholic church?

On the basis of our research data we have established which models of revelation are actually present in the religious consciousness of our research population. We have done so by means of a factor analysis, which groups those items (statements) of the various models of revelation that correlate with a certain hypothetical orientation or factor. This implies that respondents' scores on items belonging to a certain factor show an internal coherence. Table 1 indicates the correlations of the items with such a hypothetical orientation. If all models are present in the religious consciousness of the respondents, we should be able to find a hypothetical orientation or factor corresponding to each model. The analysis shows that not all models are present in the religious consciousness or the research population (see Table 1). In fact only four out of six models are found.

The first model, revelation as doctrine, is very clearly present in the religious consciousness of the research population. The content of this model is dominated by item A1: 'Faith refers to the deposit of divinely revealed truth' (see Table 1). This model also contains two items of the dialectical model: 'Faith has only been made possible by man's redemption by Jesus Christ' (D2) and 'Faith is only possible thanks to the biblical account of God's word' (D3). This strengthens the exclusive and absolute character of the doctrinal model.

The second model that is found in the religious consciousness of these core members is the model of revelation as history, but only in its critical version of liberation theology (see Table 1, factor 2). Therefore we will refer to this model as the model of the history of liberation rather than the model of revelation as history.

The third model is that of revelation as interpersonal encounter.

The last factor that is found consists of three items of the model of revelation as new awareness (F) and one item of the model of revelation as history (B).

42

The dominant item in this factor is: 'Faith is essential for man as a longing for infinity' (E3). The item of the historical model that is present in this model refers to the nature of history as leading to an ultimate goal (B2). This item shares a transcendental character with the items of the new awareness model. Therefore we will refer to this model as the model of revelation as transcendental awareness rather than new awareness.

Table 1: Models of revelation (factor analysis)

	F1	F2	F3	F4
Items				
A1	.76			
A2	.65			
D2	.62			
A6	.62			
A4	.61			
A5	.60			
D3	.59			
B4		.79		
B5		.76		
B6		.74		
F4			.79	
F5			.74	
F2			.74	
F1			.58	
E3				.72
E4				.65
B2				.62
E1				.55
	F1	F2	F3	F4
% of expl.				
variance	29.1%	11,7%	8,0%	6,3%

43

reliability
(alpha)   .81   .80   .70   .65

F1:   revelation as doctrine
F2:   revelation as the history of liberation
F3:   revelation as personal encounter
F4:   revelation as transcendental awareness

2) How strong is the preference for these models?
The respondents express the strongest preference for the model of revelation as interpersonal encounter. The preference for this model borders on complete acceptance (4.14). There is a high degree of consensus about this model among the respondents. The doctrinal model meets with the least acceptance (3.08). The respondents are in doubt about this model; they neither accept nor reject it.

The transcendental awareness model and the history of liberation model are accepted, although far less than the interpersonal encounter model. The preference for the history of liberation model is significantly stronger than the preference for the transcendental awareness model. The greatest dissent among the respondents concerns the history of liberation model (.81 standard deviation). Some core members strongly prefer this model, while others reject it or are in doubt.

Table 2: Preference for models of revelation (group means)

	Mean	Standard-deviation
Models of:		
– doctrine	3.08	.69
– transcendental awareness	3.30	.65
– history of liberation	3.50	.81
– interpersonal encounter	4.14	.54

N.B. scale from 1 (complete rejection) to 5 (strong preference)

3) Is there a relation between these models in the religious consciousness of core members of the Catholic church?
Correlation here means that the greater the respondents' acceptance is of one

model, the greater their acceptance is of another model. In our research all models correlate with each other except two, namely the doctrinal model and the interpersonal encounter model (see Figure 1). This means that the degree of acceptance of the doctrinal model does not correlate with the degree of acceptance of the interpersonal encounter model.

The transcendental awareness model is more strongly related to the doctrinal model (.41) than to the two other models.

The interpersonal encounter model in its turn is more strongly related to the history of liberation model (.42) than to the transcendental awareness model (.32).

FIGURE 1: Correlations (rho > .30) between models of revelation

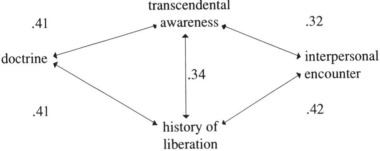

4) Who are the typical representatives of the different models of revelation? We have investigated whether some models are preferred more by people with a certain socio-cultural background than other models. We have distinguished five aspects of the socio-cultural background of core members that could be relevant in this respect, namely sex, age, the size of the town in which people live, educational level and political views. Below we will discuss the typical representatives of each model of revelation and their respective socio-cultural backgrounds.

Let us first look at the model of revelation as doctrine. Our research shows that we typically find this model among two groups: older people and women. The older people are, the greater their acceptance of this model. We can distinguish three age groups. Core members older than 50 accept this model (average 3.22). People between 30 and 50 neither accept nor reject it. Core members younger than 30 reject the doctrinal model (2.54). We can also see that women tend to accept the doctrinal model (3.24). Men neither accept nor reject it.

For the transcendental awareness model no typical representatives could be found. In other words, the acceptance of this model is not related to particular aspects of the socio-cultural background of core members.

We typically find the history of liberation model among women, highly-educated people and people with left-wing political views. Women show a significantly stronger preference for this model than men (3.74 against 3.43). Core members with an academic degree also show a stronger preference for the history of liberation model than people with little education. Also people with left-wing sympathies show a stronger preference for this model than conservative people.

Finally, also with the interpersonal encounter model we see that people's political views affect their acceptance of the model. Left-wing core members show a very strong preference for this model (4.43). Conservative people show a significantly lower degree of acceptance of this model, although they still tend to accept it (3.98).

5) Is the preference for a specific model influenced by an heteronomous or autonomous attitude towards religion?
People with an autonomous attitude towards religion want to form their own judgement about the truth of certain beliefs; they want to develop a religious identity that is in harmony with their own conceptions. People with a heteronomous attitude tend to take over the religious beliefs that are handed down to them; they want to base their beliefs on the doctrine of the Church.

The respondents in our research strongly prefer an autonomous attitude (4.18). They are not sure whether to accept or reject a heteronomous attitude (3.15). It is important to notice that there is a very weak, but positive correlation between these two attitudes (rho .20). Apparently it is not a matter of choosing either autonomy or heteronomy for the core members. Both attitudes can go together (Hermans & van der Ven 1993).

Does a heteronomous or autonomous attitude influence these core members' acceptance of a specific model of revelation? It does, but this influence takes different forms (see Table 3). There are two models that are exclusively influenced by heteronomy, namely the model of revelation as doctrine and as transcendental awareness. Also there are two models that are influenced both by heteronomy and by autonomy, namely the model of revelation as the history of liberation and as interpersonal encounter. On the history of liberation model the influence of both attitudes is almost equally strong. Finally, the influence of autonomy on the interpersonal encounter model is twice as strong as the influence of heteronomy (beta .29 against .14).

Table 3: Influence of heteronomy and autonomy on the acceptance of models of revelation (regression analysis)

	Heteronomy (beta)	Autonomy (beta)	Percentage of expl. variance
Models			
- doctrine	.53	–	.28
- transcendental awareness	.29	–	.08
- history of liberation	.18	.14	.05
- interpersonal encounter	.14	.29	.12

5. Conclusions

In this section we will first discuss the research results against the background of revelation theology. Secondly, we will go into the problem of religious socialisation in modern society. What insights do the research results provide into the content of religious socialisation?

5.1 Theology of revelation
In our discussion we will deal with the different models one by one.
- In the first place we have seen that not all models of revelation are present in the religious consciousness of core members of the Catholic church. The typology on which we based our research distinguishes six different models. However, only four of these are actually found in the religious consciousness of our respondents: doctrine, history, new (or transcendental) awareness and interpersonal encounter. A model that is not found among our research population is unlikely to be present in the minds of people. This is because we may expect core members of the church to have a clearly developed identity as Christians. If a model of revelation is present in the process of religious socialisation of Catholic people, it should be possible to assess its presence in the religious consciousness of these core members. Moreover, all our respondents follow a pastoral course for lay volunteers in Catholic parishes. Although revelation

theology as such is not a part of this course, we presume that these volunteers are capable of some reflection about faith.

- The model of revelation as dialectical presence is not present as an independent model, but some items of this model have been integrated into the model of revelation as doctrine. These items fit in with the exclusive and absolute character of the doctrinal model. To state it more bluntly: although from a historical point of view the first Vatican Council and Barth were opponents when it came to their conceptions of revelation, in a fundamental way they are alike, in that they share a positivistic view of revelation (Eicher 1977, 243). This view consigns revelation to the past. Faith is considered to be the blind acceptance of revelation as it took place in the past. The content of this model is in harmony with a heteronomous attitude. The acceptance of the doctrinal model by church members is exclusively determined by their heteronomous attitude towards faith. In this context faith is based on the acceptance of some authority, whether this is Scripture, doctrinal authority or God's truth.

- The model of revelation as inner experience is not present in the religious consciousness of Catholic church members. Characteristics of this model are the immediacy of the experience of the divine, the transformative character of this experience (making a person see himself in a new light) and the scriptural, non-doctrinal character of revelation. This model may be present among Protestant church members or in Evangelical circles. However, it seems to be no reality within the minds of Catholic believers.

- In the model of revelation as history we distinguished two aspects: a reflective and an active aspect. The reflective aspect refers to the nature of history as leading to an ultimate goal. This future fulfilment gives meaning to the present. The active aspect refers to processes of liberation in which people are actively involved with a view to the future fulfilment of the Kingdom of God. On the basis of the research results it seems arguable to consider both aspects as belonging to the same model of revelation. The historical model as it is present in the religious consciousness of the Catholic core members in our research contains only the active aspect. In this light it would be more correct to speak of the model of revelation as the history of liberation rather than of the model of revelation as history. The research results provide an answer to a question which was raised by Dulles (1983, p. 29): Will liberation theology be able to articulate a distinctive theology of revelation? The answer is: yes.

48

- The model of revelation as new awareness is strongly dominated by item E3: 'Faith is essential for man as a longing for infinity.' This model contains one item of the reflective aspect of the historical model (B2). This item shares a transcendental nature with the other items in this model. This seems to be the reason why it is present. However, it plays a minor role in the context of this model, which focuses on a reflection on man as being essentially open to revelation and faith. Therefore we prefer to refer to this model as the model of revelation as transcendental awareness, which seems to fit in better with its content. Both Dulles and Eicher see this model as a break-through for autonomy (see section 3.1). On the basis of our research results this thesis is questionable. The acceptance of this model is exclusively determined by a heteronomous attitude. How could this be explained? The essence of this model is a reflection on the transcendental basis of faith, which is seen as an innate potential of humankind. Man is fundamentally open to transcendence (Rahner 1976, p. 174). This gives faith a natural basis. There is a correspondence between this openness and Christian revelation. Man's questions correspond with the answers of revelation, but these answers are not within man's reach. They are presented by God's self-revelation in Christ. Does this not make people passive recipients of revelation? Does this not put us ultimately in a heteronomous position?

- The interpersonal encounter model is most strongly determined by the autonomous attitude. This is underlined by the fact that there is no correlation between this model and the model of revelation as doctrine. However, it is important to note that this model is not solely influenced by autonomy. As in the history of liberation model, autonomy and heteronomy go together here. We are not just dealing with an autonomous subject who creates his own faith. A creative element and a receptive element seem to go hand in hand in these models, especially in the history of liberation model. Perhaps this is the most balanced model of revelation that is present in our time.

5.2 Religious Socialisation

In revelation theology the fundament of faith is reflected upon. What is the nature of faith? The problem of religious socialisation is not only a problem of changing doctrines or disappearing religious practices. As a result of the process of modernisation, faith itself is questioned. Are religion and modern culture not mutually exclusive? If not, what kind of faith is in harmony with modern culture? What light do the research results throw on these questions?

– First of all, it is important to note that the four models that are present in the religious consciousness of core members of the Catholic church, have been successfully internalised. These core members have integrated these models into their identity as Christians. In other words, the religious socialisation of Catholic church members is explicitly and implicitly based on these models.

– The model of revelation as doctrine is losing ground. We typically find this model among older people. The degree of acceptance of this model shows a gulf between different age groups. People over 50 accept this model; people between 30 and 50 are in doubt; church members under 30 reject this model. In the Catholic church the second Vatican Council paved the way for a new model of revelation. Church members who are now over 50 were over 20 when the second Vatican Council started. In their youth they were fully socialised on the basis of the model of revelation as doctrine. The group of church members under 30 were born after the second Vatican Council. The age group between 30 and 50 grew up in the years of transition. This clearly seems to indicate that the model of revelation as doctrine is losing its impact in the religious socialisation of Catholics. This model does not take hold in the generation of young Catholics who are now being socialised. In other words, if this model forms the essence of all the efforts made by various agents of religious socialisation, there is little hope of success.

– The doctrinal model is predominantly found among women rather than men. The question is if the process of religious socialisation may be influenced by the socialisation of women. Characteristic of the doctrinal model is blind obedience to an authority. Is this not characteristic of the socialisation of women in our western culture? Could there be an 'uneasy alliance' between these two processes of socialisation? If so, does this not make it necessary for socialising agents to be critical of this alliance?

– At the same time women are typical representatives of the liberation model. This can be interpreted in at least two different ways. The first interpretation again has to do with the socialisation of women. Are women not socialised to be caring in our culture? Are they not taught to efface themselves and be prepared to help others? Or is it so that women have a different ethical approach from men, in which a caring orientation is central (Gilligan 1982)? This commitment to others is characteristic of the history of liberation model. The second explanation could be connected with the fact that women are conscious of belonging to the oppressed, who are central in this model. Women know what it is like to be oppressed. This may account for their greater acceptance of this model.

– The model of revelation as transcendental awareness seems to meet with little acceptance among church members. As is the case with the doctrinal model, this model is solely influenced by heteronomy. The question is whether this model is an adequate answer to the problems raised by the process of modernisation. If not, is it wise to focus on this model in religious socialisation?

– The two models that are most in harmony with modern culture are the model of revelation as the history of liberation and as interpersonal encounter. These are the models that meet with the greatest acceptance among core members of the Catholic church. Apparently religious socialisation has been most successful in handing down these conceptions of revelation and faith. This success could be accounted for by the balance between heteronomy and autonomy which characterises these models. People are recipients of a tradition that is handed down to them, but at the same time this tradition leaves room for their own judgment about the truth of what is being handed down. This opens the door for communication about faith. Without communication religious socialisation stagnates (Van der Slik 1992). The models of revelation as the history of liberation and as interpersonal encounter seem to lay the strongest foundation for the content of religious socialisation in our modern culture.

Literature

Dulles, A. (1983). Models of Revelation. Dublin: Gill and Macmillan.

Eicher, P. (1976). Offenbarung. Zur Präzisierung einer überstrapazierten Kategorie. In: G.Bitter & G.Miller (ed.). Konturen heutiger Theologie. München: Kösel, pp. 108-134.

Eicher, P. (1977). Offenbarung. Prinzip neuzeitlicher Theologie. München: Kösel.

Gilligan, C. (1982). In a Different Voice. Psychological Theory and Woman's Development. Cambridge M.A.: Harvard U.P.

Gutierrez, G. (1974). Theologie van de bevrijding. Baarn: Ten Have.

Habermas, J. (1981). Theorie des kommunikativen Handelns. Bd. I/II. Frankfurt.

Hermans, C.A.M. & J.A. van der Ven (1993). Katechese in het perspectief van de Verlichting. Doeloriëntaties in de volwassenenkatechese. in: Praktische Theologie (20)1, 3-27.

Kaufmann, F.X. & G. Stachel (1980). Religiöse Socialisation. In: F.Böckle et al. (ed.). Christlicher Glaube in moderner Gesellschaft. Bd.25, Freiburg/ Basel/ Wien: Herder, pp. 117-164.

Levinas, E. (1980). Dialog. In: F. Böckle et al. (ed.). Christlicher Glaube in moderner Gesellschaft. Bd.1, Freiburg/ Basel/ Wien: Herder, pp. 61-85.

McFague, S. (1987). Models of God. Theology for a Nuclear Age. London.

Pannenberg, W. (1971). Theologie und Reich Gottes. Gütersloh.

Rahner, K. (1976). Grundkurs des Glaubens. Einführung in den Begriff des Christentums. Freiburg/ Basel/ Wien: Herder.

Schillebeeckx, E. (1980). Erfahrung und Glaube. In: F.Böckle et al. (ed.). Christlicher Glaube in moderner Gesellschaft. Bd.25, Freiburg/ Basel/ Wien: Herder, pp. 73-116.

Schreuder, O. (1985). Religie en modernisering. In: L.Laeyendecker & O.Schreuder. Religie en politiek. Verkenningen op een spanningsveld. Kampen: KOK, pp. 117-130.

Seckler, M. (1980). Auklärung und Offenbarung. In: F.Böckle et al. (ed.). Christlicher Glaube in moderner Gesellschaft. Bd.21, Freiburg/ Basel/ Wien: Herder, pp. 5-78.

Seckler, M. (1985). Der Begriff der Offenbarung. In: W.Kern, H.-J. Pottmeyer & M. Seckler (ed.). Handbuch der Fundamentaltheologie. Freiburg/ Basel/ Wien: Herder, pp. 60-83.

Slik, F.W.P. van der (1992). Overtuigingen, attituden, gedrag en ervaringen. Een onderzoek naar de godsdienstigheid van ouders en van hun kinderen. Diss. Tilburg.

Stark, R. & Ch.Y. Glock (1968). American Piety. The Nature of Religious Commitment. Berkely: Un. of California Press.

IV Religious Socialisation and the Identification of Religion

Hans-Georg Ziebertz

In general, religious socialisation is regarded as a process that introduces children and young people into the tradition of the Christian faith and instructs them in this faith. In the following article on this subject, we concentrate on questions about the context of 'secondary socialisation' at school (1).[1] In today's literature there are many attemps to redetermine the place of religion in modern society. It turns out that the secularisation theorem with the adopted polarity between faith and faithless is inadequate as a model of explanation (2). There are many who think that the modernisation theorem is better equipped for grasping the present manifestation of religion (3). This manifestation contains a phenomenon, 'religious syncretism' (4), which has hardly been noticed by religion-pedagogical efforts until this moment. It presents new challenges to religion-pedagogical efforts (5). The path of considerations runs from a more social-scholarly analysis towards the interests of religious teaching.

1. The indicated In-tolerance of Religion and the Modern Ones

'The controversy about religious teaching in school refuses to settle down, on the contrary, the confusion among the contending parties is worse than before. Representatives of a practical, realistic world view, solely concentrating on life on earth, as well as those men, to whom religion is the innermost, most private cult of the heart, demand its complete elimination from the school curriculum. Yet, more than ever before, the state sides with the church, which is still in control of the curriculum, due to its traditional, partly archaic and, more often than not, unchildlike ideas. …It seems that there is only one way to guarantee a satisfactory further development of the school in this field – we shall have to direct religious teaching towards neutral territory.'[2]

Thus, the board for school reform argues in Bremen in 1905. To a large

---

1. Whenever specific questions about the school system are discussed, I have particulary in mind the German context.
2. 'Erklärung der Vereinigung für Schulreform' (1905); in: F. Gansberg (Hg.), Religionsunterricht? Achtzig Gutachten. Leipzig 1906, V-VIII

extent, religious teaching is regarded as being 'incompatible' with the modern nature of school and society. Religion, at least its claim to a comprehensive world interpretation and an organisation of action, seems to be incompatible with modern requirements. One of the spokesmen at that time, the educationalist Fritz Gansberg from Bremen, writes:

'The metaphysical veil is lifted in front of the growing, investigating and creating human mind. Christianity no longer encompasses life, indeed, life of mankind, which is becoming richer and more profound, has started to expel Christianity. Christianity is a sinking world. Does the school intend to offer resistance to this process of development? Does it wish to rescue what is past saving? ...Religious teaching should therefore be removed!'[3]

The diagnosis of this view at the time is unmistakable: religion and the modern ones do not agree with one another. Modern stands for 'progress' and 'change'; religion, however, in the social form of Christianity, opposes progress. Fate seems to have decided that religion already is, or will before long have become, a marginal factor in society. A normative communication on religion at school is regarded as being out-of-date. The only alternative left is historical-comparative religious teaching, which drops the claim on religious education.

These discussions in the state of Bremen indeed resulted in an alternative model of teaching biblical history.[4] And although criticism on established denominational religious teaching has only temporarily died down ever since, in order to burst out again with vehemence[5] (as, for instance, during the 68th period, when the state and its neutral world view caused a discussion in favour of removing religious teaching from schools), it was not until recently that there was yet another decision, involving a fundamental structural change of religious teaching in Germany (in the federal state of Brandenburg). Without entering at length into this incident here, it should be observed, that there has been an evident change in public opinion. It was not a political fight against religious teaching, which resulted in an alternative model of teaching, but the opposite, really: the fact that questions about religion should also be discussed at school, is matter on which almost all parties agree.

At this stage, it is interesting to look at the social-historical background, against which this new discussion on the subject of religious teaching takes

---

3. cfr. ebd., XIf.
4. cfr. M. Spieß, Religionsunterricht oder nicht?; in: J. Lott, Religion – Warum und wozu in der Schule?, Weinheim 1992, 81-102
5. cfr. G. Otto, Schule und Religion. Eine Zwischenbilanz in weiterführender Absicht, Hamburg 1972

place. It appears that the changing role of Christian religion within our society, or rather, secularisation, but also an increased awareness of a difference between religion on the one hand, and ecclesiastical Christianity on the other hand, cause major problems to religious teaching. Franz Xaver Kaufmann gets to the heart of the matter where the present situation is concerned, by stating that it is difficult to distinguish between religion and Christianity organized by the church in Germany. It is much more common to regard ecclesiastical Christianity (alone) responsible for religion.[6] After all, established denominational religious teaching, as it still exists in Germany, has also sprung from this understanding. There seems to be an increasing awareness that we find ourselves in a period of transition, without knowing where it will end. Yet, what are these changes and how can they be explained, theoretically?

The following considerations show, that the tension existing between 'religious' and 'secular' within the secularization theorem, fail as a way to characterize the modern ones. Accordingly, the religion-pedagogical difficulties cannot be blamed on the virtuosity of the theologian alone, in order to build the correlative bridge between secular experience and religious meaning. Nowadays, religion-pedagogical efforts more often take place on the stage of a cultural religious variety, to which, the tendency within the secularisation way of thinking towards marginalisation of the Christian faith, no longer seems to be the only possible reality. Many people have released Christianity organized by the church, as well as professional theology from the 'exclusive qualification' in questions about religion. They take their religious interests into their own hands and create an individual model of subjective religiosity.

2. The Boundaries of the Secularisation Diagnosis

Many impulses that describe the position of the Christian faith and its social forms against the background of contemporary development, fall back on the concept of secularisation as a theoretical explanatory framework. Despite the fact that the many interpretations of this concept have been worked out more than once, in theological terminology one often comes across the connotation, which notices that both Christianity and the church have been exposed to a linearly running process of decline, ever since the Enlightenment. Ecclesias-tical-sociological research appears to supply enough of the appropriate material. By means of the common parameters, such as 'education of members', 'church attendance', 'baptism', 'Communion- and confirmation

---

6. cfr. F.X. Kaufmann, Religion und Modernität, Tübingen 1989, 2

participation', 'church weddings', 'changes in religion, or in whatever it is that people believe in', 'Decline in the willingness of parents to bring up their children in a religious way' and the like, it becomes clear that an almost continuous decline stands out, which not only takes place in the cities, but also in the country. Within the framework of this entrance into reality, secularisation indicates a triple process of decay[7]:

* in the first place, a decline of the plausibility of the Christian faith as a whole,
* secondly, the erosion of Christian consciousness and
* thirdly, the decline in the participation in Christian performances.

Within Europe, Germany ranks as one of the most secularized countries, together with Denmark anf the Netherlands.

This process has its effect on the religious teaching we are familiar with: most pupils are only marginally acquainted with the Christian faith and the complementarity between life in school and in the congregation still exists in only a few cases; to a large extent, families drop out as bodies of primary religious education and as a result, the unasked-for conformity between school and parental home concerning religious educational goals is no longer natural. The problem of teaching has become incalculable, when taking children and young people into a religious conceptual universe, the elements of which they can often no longer fit into their life structure, because there is neither a familial nor a social basic structure. Several teachers have already, in fact, accepted the consequence, and are sure to approach the subject of religious teaching in an informative-descriptive, phenomenological or historical way, at least, no longer primarily aim for a confirmation in their introduction of religious faith.[8] Is it not therefore justified to speak of the marginalisation of religion in our society, and does it not inevitably mark the end of the possibility of any religious teaching in school?

When following the consequences arising from the discussion on secularisation, the situation is indeed discouraging. It remains to be seen whether this observation is complete. It is true that one can refer to corresponding empirical proofs, but they only sustain whatever has been considered as possible results in the system of categories of the researchers.

---

7. cfr. J.A. van der Ven, Kontingenz und Religion in einer säkularisierten und multikulturellen Gesellschaft; in: J.A. van der Ven/H.-G. Ziebertz (ed.), Religiöser Pluralismus und Interreligiöses Lernen, Weinheim/Kampen 1994, 15-37

8. cfr. H.-G. Ziebertz, Religiöse Lernprozesse und Interreligiöses Bewußtsein; in: J.A. van der Ven/H.-G. Ziebertz (ed.), Religiöser Pluralismus und Interreligiöses Lernen, Weinheim/Kampen 1994, 277-289

Critical questions are therefore aimed less at the results, but at the completeness of the research perspectives. After all, the more restricted the explanatory model is on which the research has been based, the lower is the actual explanatory quality.

Recently, questions of this nature have been asked more than once, and it is worthwhile to test their validity.[9] They aim at the suitability of the concept of secularisation as a theoretical explanatory model for the historically understandable events that have been mentioned. Its suitability is questioned, as processes of revitalization are visible besides the undeniable symptoms of erosion of religion, which – even when they do not occur on a broader scale and not necessarily lead to a re-establishment of the tradition – contradict, at any rate, the thesis of a linear-causal running disolution of religion.

It can furthermore be demonstrated that religious processes of change do not pass off in a static-linear way, but in a dynamic way. The meaning of religions can be on the upgrade or change and go downward or run in a fluctuating movement. Whatever holds for one particular religion, should not necessarily also apply for other religions at the same time – anyway, this is the result of research carried out by Duke and Johnson, who have analysed developments in 200 countries over a period of 80 years.[10] In perspective, this means: present developments cannot be looked upon as being irrevocable. It takes, however, closer examination to pass an appropriate judgement on the tendency of secularisation on the one hand and the portion of revitalization.

Thomas Luckmann already prepared this way of understanding about 30 years ago. He came to the conclusion that religion can not only be identified as a complex of images of the hereafter, but, in accordance with the tradition of Durkheim, appears as a socialization of the individual in the objectification of subjective experiences, or in the sense of protection, as a matter which exceeds (transcends) the obviousness of a direct experience in one's present life.

This kind of broad functional concept of religion is, no doubt, the basis of the problem that all 'worldly world views' could be raised to the status of a religion. The specific religious aspect, recognizable by contents,

---

9.   cfr. Kaufmann 1989, a.a.O.; K. Gabriel, Christentum zwischen Tradition und Postmoderne, Freiburg 1992
10.   cfr. J. van der Lans, Religiöse Universalien in der Psychologie des Selbst; in: J.A. van der Ven/H.-G. Ziebertz (ed.), Religiöser Pluralismus und Interreligiöses Lernen, Weinheim/Kampen 1994, 71-85

respectively only by substance, according to criticism, is openly condemned.[11] On the other hand, it can be useful in the sense of a broadening of perspective, to pursue this definition for a moment, in order to understand the spectre of 'contents of beliefs' and 'social forms', at all, that have a religious function. In the case of a search for forms of expression of individual religiosity, it is not about the construction of a counter concept for ecclesiastically established religion and piety, but merely about the consciousness of the subjective formation of available world views.

3. Modernization as an Explanatory Framework for Religious Processes of Change

In this sense, the diagnosis of decline connected with the secularisation theorem, has lost persuasiveness in the religion-socioligical discussion and has given way to the 'concept of modernization'. Modernization is not, as has been mentioned at the beginning, a concept of future-oriented fighting against tradition and status-quo, but an analytical category. The question is, how modernization takes place and what effect it has on religion, or better still: what its destructive and productive effects are like. In the latest comprehensive portayal of Gabriel [12], modernization is put down in three separate processes in relation with religion – I wish to give a rough outline of them:

1) modernization as a process of religious individualization
'religious individualization' is regarded as an inevitable consequence of social processes of differentiation, allowing an individual to partake in parallel different atmospheres of action. Religious individualization takes place in social consistencies, to which – at the time when religious social environments were in operation – were attributed religious dimensions. The traditionally applicable interpretation of life has been deprived of its universal validity: it has become an option – one *can* be in favour of it. Values, such as religious freedom and individual autonomy are radicalized, they define the modern portayal of man, if necessary, also at a distance of ecclesiastically institutionalized religion.

2) Modernization as a process of de-institutionalization of religious institutions.
De-institutionalization means that the institutionalized Christian religion of

---

11. cfr. H. Knoblauch, Die Verflüchtigung der Religion ins Religiöse; in: Th. Luckmann, Die unsichtbare Religion, Frankfurt 1991, 7-41; A. Feige, Zwischen universaler Religionstheorie und theologisch bestimmter Kirchlichkeitsforschung; in: Sociologica Internationalis 30(1992)2, 143-157
12. cfr. Gabriel 1992, a.a.O.

the size known to us, is no longer able to bind religious orientations and statements of value. In the first place, it contains the impairment of the justification, that is, the naturalness and doubtlessness of an institution (which is not the same as the public effect of Christianity); secondly, the de-monopolization of religion, regarding the joining together of expressions of life in a model of unity (recognizable by the permanent presence of religious minorities, the attraction of non-Christian religions, for Christians, New Age, etc., as well); thirdly, as the reduction of mechanisms of social control, making the distance to institutionalized religion possible without the danger of any sanctions; in the fourth place, as a withdrawal of the institution in the sense of a limitation of formal control (as far as the differentiation and pluralization of social forms allow) and in the fifth place, as an impairment, respectively, collapse of religious socialization events. The latter is indicated by the increasing difficulty to pass on institutionally defined beliefs to the next generation. In connection with this, Gabriel reaches the conclusion, which is meaningful for religion pedagogics:

'We should take for granted that a religious-ecclesiastical socialization, in the sense of passing on ecclesiastical constituents of knowledge, norms and beliefs is only possible within a minority of clearly under 10 percent.'[13]

3) Modernization as a process of religious cultural pluralization of religion and Christianty
The analysis has Gabriel conclude that, in the first place, it is justified to speak of secularization, in the sense of the hypothesis of marginalization, respectively, collapse, though not as a process covering all, but as a separate process within modernization, supported by other separate processes of re-ligious-productive movements. Especially the effects of modernization concerning content, are of interest in connection with our theme.

4. Consequences of Modernization: Subjective Formation of Syncretism

According to Gabriel, religious individuality on the one hand, and impairment of the institutional binding power of ecclesiastical Christianity on the other hand, result in a radicalized pluralism of religious systems of meaning in all, and in a pluralization within Christianity itself. Religious pluralism means, *in the first place*, that there is a variety of religious forms, which are only partly dominated by institutional examples of Christianity and, *secondly*, that this variety is (no more) embedded in social environments.

The cultural examples of a diffuse Christianity and religiosity, appearing besides more traditional Christianity, are mainly comprehensible, by means

---

13. cfr. ebd. 149

of the things they do *not* have in common with more explicit Christianity.

At any rate, they are not comprehensible in the sense of an alternative, in essence, coherent world view, opposing Christian religion.[14] There is neither a simple shift of the social place of religion, away from its primary institution: the new forms are not simply the 'hidden church' or 'ecclesia vera atque invisibilis'.[15]

In addition, the territories of specific Christianity part, meaning that the *social cultural examples* and the *individual forms of religion* release themselves of the *institutional Christianity with its rules and regulations* and are hardly connected with one another anymore, by means of communicative processes of exchange and mediation. Volker Drehsen points out: 'The diversification of religious phenomena is linked with moments of erasure of society as a whole, particularly with the consequences of social-cultural differentiation and complexity, felt to be threatening to individuality. Thus, conditions have been established, demanding the formation of a form of syncretism.'[16]

First of all, we are dealing with a functional disentanglement and emancipation of the sectors forming society (politics, science, culture...), which perform all central functions for society, though are no longer encompassed by a religious justification, but are rather based on a rationality of their own (social differentiation). In connection with this, the *formation of syncretism* is a result of the neutralization of politics, economics, etc., by means of which, the potential increases of possibilities for combinations of connections of value and action.

On the other hand, the religious field itself experiences a internal differentiation (functional differentiation) of the system. A great many structures of production, mediation and acquisition are developed in between experienced and acquired religion.

The *formation of syncretism* appears to be the emancipation from systematic claims of consistence, found to be unacceptable.

If one is inclined to regard the formation of sycretism, not as an indicator of secularization, but as a sign of religious activity (namely, as an activity,: 'to achieve relational ties between, in themselves, disparate goals in life')[17], then where does this activity get its drive of motivation? The answer to this is, that this motivation can be found in the ambivalence of the modern ones

---

14.   cfr. Knoblauch, a.a.O., 26
15.   cfr. Knoblauch, a.a.O., 28
16.   cfr. V. Drehsen, Die Anverwandlung des Fremden; in: J.A. van der Ven/H.-G. Ziebertz (ed.), Religiöser Pluralismus und Interreligiöses Lernen, Weinheim/Kampen 1994, 39-69
17.   A. Feige, Jugend und Religiosität; in: Aus Politik und Zeitgeschichte B41-42/93 v. 8.10.1993, 3-8

themselves. After all, although on the one hand, the variety of forms of social differentiation allow the individual more freedom and space to move in, they also complicate the creation of a meaning of life as a whole, which should be such, that it has a supporting power enclosing all differentiated separate fields, the individual moves in. Neither society as a whole, nor its differentiated parts are capable of creating this unity in the development of a meaning of life.

However, the churches have also lost their monopoly claim to the explanation of the world and the meaning of life. There are three results: the creation of meaning is no longer the other side of institutional pretexts, but has become a personal occasion (1); it is true that there are still objective pretexts of meaning of the Christian church – they are frequently still consulted first – but their acceptance is the result of a free choice, instead of an automatic one (2); as to contents, questions about meaning concentrate on themes about leading one's own life (3).

Consequently, the 'religion-productive' side of this development, in the sense of a new need for religion, can be seen in the 'systematically-produced surplus of contingents' (Gabriel), so that also *as one of the last certainties of the modern myth of progress...the conviction of a future without religion has fallen victim to the process of de-enchantment'.*[18] Particularly the obstacle of developing an interpretation of the meaning of life and the world, at all, which will forever have an impact on one's life, stimulates the search for religion. The strong need for an individual and social triumph over contingence, can be seen, individually, within the framework of the victory over fear and life, where the subjective experience itself, such as listening carefully to the transcendence of one's own self, has a religious character. From a social point of view, religion serves to experience the world as a meaningful whole.[19] Nevertheless: both emphases point out that the 'new religious' examples of interpretation and ritual practices that make their appearance, are independent of the traditional Christian religion and connect both new-religious and also Christian elements, and are, thus, not simply identical with the customary Christian tradition.[20] This 'new religiosity' remains at a distance from those established social forms of religion, which do not seem to guarantee this unity. Those who have dissociated themselves from them, do not easily come back.[21]

---

18.   cfr. Gabriel 1992, a.a.O., 157
19.   cfr. Cl. Bovay, Religion und Gesellschaft in der Schweiz; in: A. Dubach/R.J. Campiche (ed.), Jede(r) ein Sonderfall? Religion in der Schweiz, Zürich 1993, 211
20.   cfr. Gabriel 1992, a.a.O.
21.   cfr. Bovay 1993, a.a.O., 210

It corresponds with the possibility of 'religiosity without a church'.[22] It can result in a situation in which the genesis and the presence of such examples of culture, in which religion seems to have an activity and can be explained without the assumption of particular intended processes of socialization, whereas the processes of tradition of the Christian faith have difficulty with their crystallization and let the fear of a non-Christian society become a reality.

From the religion-psychological end, there has recently been an attempt to explain this tendency more strongly with references to invariable structural characteristics, which man has at his disposal to religious questions: the final self and the utopian passion: the self is not regarded as an individually-closed system, but as a narrator of dialogue, who is both three-dimensionally organized and personified and is a social structure, as well, so that the other one is incorporated in the self-structure. *The self functions as a room, in which the I is observing the ME and explains the movements of ME by means of narration. In one's consciousness, the I always looks upon the ME as the leading character in one's personal story of life.*[23] Since the consciousness is inevitably connected with the restriction, due to the three-dimensional self-experience, the dialogue can get stuck with itself – the deadlock appears at moments of final questions about the meaning of life. Johann Baptist Metz has once characterized 'interruption' as the shortest definition of religion.[24] The second structural characteristic is, according to Van der Lans, the 'utopian passion': the hope for 'better times', hoping to be able to start again after a failure, hoping to be able to cross the enforced and daily noticeable limits and restrictions and to anticipate a new reality in one's imagination. Symbolizations come up in the passion to triumph over gravity or to be caught by light. All religions have these symbolizations, and empirical research has shown that they are also found in the day-dreams of young people, especially during their adolescence, when the young are focussed on themselves and become aware of the contingency. According to Durkheim, utopian passion and religious life come together, when religion takes into consideration the need to raise man above himself and allow him to lead a higher life, which would not be possible on the mere basis of spontaneous inspiration. Religion helps people to express these utopian passions in a symbolic way.

---

22. cfr. V. Drehsen 1994, a.a.O.
23. cfr. J.A. van der Lans 1994, a.a.O.
24. J.B. Metz, Unterbrechungen. Theologisch-politische Perspektiven und Profile, Gütersloh 1981

These signs can help theologians, first of all, to understand the situation, in which the tradition of sociological or psychological theories on religion is no longer visible, as an functional explanation of religion. Instead, it is stated that religion (also) has a function for people, which becomes visible in people's need for an explanation of the meaning of life and identity.[25] This explains the remaining association with religion and characterizes the present challenge to theology and religion pedagogics.

5. Challenges for Religion Pedagogics

From the above-mentioned considerations, one should bear in mind that the thesis of the marginalization of religion needs differentiation. Besides atheism and religious indifference, a scattered religious field has been created, which can certainly not count as an indication of the end of religion, but, on the contrary, also signifies an *interest in religion*. For that matter, it cannot be the end of the occupation with religion, either. However, the new-religious interest largely takes place outside of the ecclesiastical framework. Special about this 'new-religiosity', which is difficult to grasp for theologians like ourselves, is its syncretistic regulation: elements of the Christian religion are seen as compatible with notions, symbols and rites of non-Christian religiosity; they are mixed, rearranged, completely or partially replaced, without experiencing the criteria of the theology of revelation, dogmatic or even ecclesiastically-normative criteria as an obstacle. This corresponds with findings by Andreas Feige, when he states that on the one hand, a religion laid down by others is individually ignored and on the other hand, there is a need for a 'practice of an everyday-aesthetic religiosity which is individually and emotionally livable', without there being a connection with a claim to a consistent theo=logical agreement.[26] In this respect, the syncretic perspective distinguishes itself from rejecting or indifferent attitudes towards religion: it does not excavate 'security graves' towards the Christian religion, nor believes it should justify its distance to it. The possibility of a 'broadly' founded religious consumption without any social fears is much more likely. Certain forms of New Age, occultism or esotericism – research among the young makes this clear – are not regarded as a *substitute* for Christian-religious convictions, but connected *with them* in various compositions.

When discussing the faith and non-faith polarization, the personal Christian religious legitimization (the monopoly) is not under debate. It is more likely to conclude that people turn away from religion or become indifferent

---

25. cfr. J.A. van der Ven 1994, a.a.O.
26. cfr. A. Feige 1993, a.a.O., 5

towards it: on this side, faith and on the other side indifference or rejection.

On the other hand, the new-religious situation results in more questions about the monopoly position of the church over religion, since, within the sphere of religion, religious pluralism becomes a fact in our consciousness. People can appropriate Christian-religious symbols or representations, without building a relation with the monopoly bearer'. In full accordance with this, Friedrich Schweitzer diagnoses: *'A decline in church support does not correspond with a parallel drop in religious interest... Yet, there is no doubt that the influence of religion without any ties to a church is growing, whereas devotion remaims precarious.'*[27]

When considering religious teaching in Germany against this background, it is obvious that, until well into the sixties, it was a reflection of a situation, in which the two large religions – in fact, since the Reformation – held an unlimited religious monopoly.[28] 'Religion outside of the church' was not even a matter for debate for religion-sociologists.[29] Religion passed on by a church, was to be a 'religion suitable for civilized society', and the fact that the church would be co-reponsible for teaching 'religion' was far less a problem to critics, than whether this subject should be accepted in the curriculum, at all.

In view of the population of pupils during religious teaching, the Würzburg synod in 1974, no longer mentioned 'pupils with faith'[30], although people had – from a church perspective – the spectre 'faith vs. atheism/indifference' in mind. Since the eighties, it has become clear that, in view of the individual organization of faith, the monopoly of the church is losing power. This makes it difficult to change the basic assumption of religious teaching as a 'church at school', and still continue to link catechetic and proclamation-oriented expectations to it.[31][32]

---

27. F. Schweitzer, Kaum noch kirchliche Bindung. Religion und Kirche im Spiegel neuer Jugendstudien; in: Lutherische Monatshefte 32(1993)10, 19

28. D. Stoodt, Warum Religionsunterricht? Warum Sozialisationsbegleitung?; in: J. Lott 1992, a.a.O., 285-299

29. cfr. J. Matthes, Auf der Suche nach dem 'Religiösen'; in: Sociologica Internationalis 29(1991)2, 129-142

30. W. Nastainczyk, Der Synodenbeschluß zum Religionsunterricht – Geschichte und Zukunft; in: Sekretariat der Deutschen Bischofskonferenz (ed.), Religionsunterricht 20 Jahre nach dem Synodenbeschluß. Bonn 1993, 13-28

31. cfr. N. Mette, Religionsunterricht in nachchristlicher Gesellschaft; in: J. Lott 1992, a.a.O., 269-283

32. cfr. U. Hemel, Religionsunterricht – wohin? Aufgaben und Entwicklungsperspektiven; in: Katechetische Blätter 116(1991)11, 765-771

Against this background, new voices are heard that argue in favour of a *structural* reform of religious teaching[33]: it should carry out an adjustment of the situation, release itself from the denominational grip and organize itself in a multi-religious way, that is for instance, to pay equal attention to all religious traditions, without pursuing the claim to introduce people into a particular religious tradition. The problems that have been indicated are not solved by giving up the dominant position of the Christian religion and by the introduction of more historical-cultural existential religions or religious convictions in religious teaching. They have not been solved, and, for instance, 'equi-distance' towards all religions or 'neutrality' are neither theologically, nor pedagogically desirable and tenable as a 'teaching principle'.[34] Perhaps structural changes can dispose of some of the problems, but they also bring new problems, which can be easily demonstrated by a glance at our neighbouring countries. Therefore, in my opinion, all points into the direction of working on reforms *regarding content* under the existing structural conditions.

When Friedrich Schweitzer states that ecclesiastical-pedagogical actions can only tie in with the available religious interest among the young, by being involved with the young and by being prepared to enter into religious connections, that are meaningful to them[35], he is pleading, I think, in favour of a religious-pedagogical acquaintance with the environment of adolescents, bringing forward the available religious activa in it as an educational tool, not taking them as mere points of departure for the actual teaching content, but as the theme itself.

This could result in not just concentrating on the introduction of pupils into the complete compendium of theology – with a reduced complexity and spread over the years at school. In the discussion on elementary knowledge, started recently, there are more and more attempts at connecting the 'whole issue of faith as a fragment' with an introduction containing a stronger sense of the world of experience of the young and more in accordance with their age.[36]

---

33. An overview about different positions: H.-G. Ziebertz, Religionsunterricht in der Diskussion; in: Religionsunterricht an höheren Schulen (rhs) 36(1993)3, 186-198

34. W. Simon, Überlegungen zum Ansatz eines ökumenisch offenen katholischen Religionsunterrichts auf der Oberstufe des Gymnasiums; in: Religionsunterricht an höheren Schulen (rhs) 35(1992), 178-190

35. cfr. F. Schweitzer 1993, a.a.O.

36. cfr. K.E. Nipkow, Erwachsenwerden mit oder ohne Gott; in: Lebendige Katechese 15(1993)2, 109-114; H.A. Zwergel, Elementare Glaubensmomente und Erfahrungsspuren im Religionsunterricht; in: G. Hilger/G. Reilly (ed.), Religionsunterricht im

Besides, it was also about the re-insertion of the *discussion on education* and, thus, about working out the instructive function of religious teaching. It could result in religious teaching becoming a forum in which the variety of 'minds' can come together and a way to connect this coming together with the educational task, to make a contribution to *critical reflection*, to *orientation* and *distinction* of the 'minds'.

Whether and how it will be possible to develop forms of contact with the open questions and crises of meaning, produced in abundance by the modern ones, will be important not only for individual people, but in the long term for society at large. This question anticipates the problems of creating a personal identity and is connected with what we call 'social coherence'. On the one hand, the available religious-syncretic variety prevents the goal of religion-pedagogical interferences to be leading people back to ecclesiastical-denominational unification of world views. On the other hand, at a time of differentiation in all fields, it also prevents favouring religious syncretism when discussing questions about religion.

What choice is there, when the variety of forms of religiosity cannot be simply traced back to religious knowledge that has been passed on by the church, and when the relativistic tendency, implicit to religious syncretism, should not be accepted as an educational-theoretical point of view?

Possibly the only means available to modern society for the formation of pluralism, on which there is far-reaching consensus, is *communication*.[37] [38]Communication is the hinge that keeps individuality and sociality together. It is *the* form of human action, for coming to an agreement on the validity and meaning of systems of the meaning of life. It is the final necessity, one can not get round. Communication contains a triple performance, which should be revealed during teaching:

(1) First of all, it stands for 'intra-personal communication': incite pupils to communicate with themselves about matters in their lives, which they experience as fragile or stable. The objective is to get more clarity about matters that concern the pupil.

Abseits?, München 1993, 43-57; D. Zilleßen, Elementarisierung theologischer Inhalte oder elementares religiöses Lernen? Ein religionspädagogischer Grundkonflikt; in: G. Hilger/G. Reilly 1993, a.a.O., 28-42; G. Lämmermann, Stufen religionsdidaktischer Elementarisierung; in: Jahrbuch der Religionspädagogik Bd.6 (1989), Neukirchen-Vluyn 1990, 79-91; E. Feifel, Zur Konfessionalität des Religionsunterrichts; in: Lebendige Katechese 15(1993), 95-102

37. cfr. J.A. van der Ven, Ekklesiologie in Context, Kampen 1993
38. F. Strolz, 'Alternative' Religiosität: Alternative Wozu?; in: Schweizerische Zeitschrift für Soziologie 3(1991), 659-666

(2) Secondly, it means 'inter-personal communication': questions about the meaning of life are taken out of their privacy and reintegrated into social connections, teaching pupils to form and communicate their own orientation in words and to reconstruct at the same time communications from others and to relate to them, that is, to take a stand.

(3) Thirdly, it means 'inter-generative communication', in which the individual experiences that have been communicated, are taken out of their horizontal structure and put into a vertical one, which means that they are linked with the past and the future, that they are confronted with experiences and promises, passed on to us by tradition, including the Christian-ecclesiastical one. Children and adolescents should be able to learn about the various traditions of worldly wisdom that exist in our culture. They ought to know what people from the past used to believe in and what other people believe in – in this world that is growing together. They should bring about a critical exchange of ideas between the messages of the religions, especially of the Christian faith closest to us, and the new-religious syncretisms, mostly without any contents, in order to be able to accentuate their own judgement.

In these three performances, communication is not an instrument for another purpose, but by means of its realization, it is a moment of educational action itself. The problem of religious teaching, the heterogeneity of religious orientations and points of departure, becomes a theme itself. However, not for an affirmative-non-critical reason. This could mean that one should reinforce the tendency to reduce religion functionally to interests, that cannot 'conquer the rest' and to regard 'religion as merchandise', which, as the sociologist Fritz Strolz rightly remarks, is focussed on short-term consumption and offers an unstable orientation, completely the opposite of 'religion as *truth*'. It would be fatal from a theological and also an educational-theoretical point of view, if the revelation-dimensions of liberation and salvation that have been passed down, were not discussed in the communication during religious teaching. It would also be illogical to direct religious teaching towards 'neutral territory', as requested in a quotation, mentioned at the beginning. Religion would be reduced to the religiosity of the individual or to the religion of society. Opposite these two, religion that has been passed down, contains, not cleansed of metaphysical, ecstatic, utopian and eschatological elements, a critical moment. It questions, whether man can deliver himself on his own, or whether society can do this in his place.

On the basis of this, there appear to be arguments in favour of the continuation of religious teaching. Where its concept is concerned, it need not capitulate to the new challenges. Whatever is visible, is not an argument against religious teaching, but a basis for a theological and educational-theoretical new initiative.

V Death: a Core Theme in Religious Socialization

Johannes A. van der Ven

In this paper I would like to treat a theme with the help of which I am able to formulate some fundamental problems with regard to religious socialization. This theme is death. The question which I will treat reads as follows: what is the effect of religious socialization with regard to the religious meaning of death? I understand religious socialization in terms of religious education in the family and the school. In other words: to which extent does the older generation succeed to transfer the religious meaning of death to the younger one? There are some indications that this question might imply some problems, at least in the Netherlands. For instance, the percentage of dutch church members who believe in life after death decreased between 1966 and 1991 from 83% to 69% (Sociaal en cultureel rapport 1992, 458).

I would like to structure this paper in four parts. First of all I formulate the question whether the religious meaning of death can function as exemplary for religion in general and more specific for religious socialization (1). Further, I will explore the question what the effect is of religious socialization with regard to death. In order to do that, I try to find out what attitudes a specific group of young people possesses with regard to the religious meaning of death, namely university students. For that I will use the results of an empirical-theological research project that was conducted among students of the Catholic University in Nijmegen in 1990. In comparison with other youngsters these students got the most extensive religious socialization ever (2). After that I will go into the factors within religious socialization in the family and the school, that contributed to the development of those attitudes (3). Lastly, I will try to answer the question what the meaning of the research results is for developing ecclesial and pastoral policy (4).

1. Death: an Exemplary Theme?

First, I ask the question whether taking the theme of death as exemplary for religious socialization can be legitimated. Let us assume that the effect of religious socialization with regard to death is negative. If the faith in life after death belongs to the core of the Christian faith, there is reason to be worried about it. If this faith belongs to the periphery of the Christian faith, there is, perhaps, no severe problem.

1.1. Faith in life after death and the core of Christianity

In the sixties and seventies, some theologians relativized the faith in life after death. They stressed the fact that, in the bible, this faith only developed itself in later times. In connection with that, they paid attention to the textual phenomenon, that the bible, when dealing with life after death, is not concerned with giving information or dogmatic certainty about man has to expect after death. The faith in life after death in the bible is the expression of an aspiration, a longing, a hungering (Blenkinsopp 1970, 11). Some theologians were of the opinion that the person 'who is convinced that he may trust God, in fact accepts the core of the Christian faith, although he might have doubts about life after death' (Schillebeeckx 1970, 434).[1] Other theologians pointed at the discussion between the Pharisees, who accepted the resurrection, and the Sadducees, who rejected it. Against this background, some theologians interpreted the oldest eucharistic theology, which can be found in 1 Cor. 11,24-26. The apostle speaks of the commemoration of Jesus' death, without explicitly referring to the Lord's living presence after his death. From this perspective the question is asked whether there is some place not only for pharisaic Christians but also for sadducaic Christians (Schoonenberg 1969, 81; Logister 1988).

In the eighties, too, some voices made themselves heard in order to relativize the faith in life after death. Some theologians took still a further step. They were of the opinion that it was preferable to put the faith in life after death between brackets. By that the attention of the faithful could be reoriented from life after death, to life here on earth. That could provide the opportunity to interact with God in an unselfish way, without the perspective of receiving reward or punishment after death. The consequence of this is, that there no longer is an opportunity for revenge, which is implied in the idea of a final judgment for other people, opponents or enemies. It could offer the possibility to convert oneself from being a calculating bourgeois to a real believer Pohier 1977, 191ff.; 1986, 112-130).

In contrast, some voices could be heard which stressed the central importance of the faith in life after death. Tillich is of the opinion that the resurrection is the symbolic expression of the transformation of temporal life into the living with God. It is a message which belongs to the centre of the

---

1. From the perspective of the interpretation of the faith in life after death in terms of the expression of longing, the sentence 'although he might have doubts about life after death' is to be replaced by 'although he might not be longing', because 'doubting' has an informative connotation, not an aspirative one, as 'longing' has.

Christian faith (Tillich 1966, III, 414). Küng expresses himself even more impressively. For him the faith in life after death has to do with a fundamental, existential alternative, which cannot be escaped. People, according to choose between trust or mistrust in God (Küng 1982, 283).[2] In his latest book the Dutch protestant theologian Kuitert expresses himself even more sharply. He says: 'The crucial role of Jesus' resurrection in the Christian tradition is beyond dispute. If Christ has not risen, the Christian proclamation is without any meaning at all' (Kuitert 1992, 167).

1.2. An anthropological perspective

Does the faith in life after death belong to the core of the Christian faith, yes or no? Can it be interpreted in terms of an exemplary theme within religious socialization, yes or no? Is there a way out of this dilemma? In this paper, I would not like to look for support from exegetical or systematic-theological studies.[3] Here, I would like to depart from a fundamental anthropological experience that is seemingly totally unconnected with death and life after death, and that was analyzed by Aristotle and Paul Ricoeur after him: friendship.

In his Ethica Nicomacheia Aristotle distinguishes between three kinds of friendship: friendship based on the endeavour for use and profit, friendship based on the endeavour for lust and pleasure, and friendship based on the endeavour for happiness of the other person for reasons of the other person himself (book eight, ii-iii). This third kind of friendship, this intrinsic friendship, implies intimacy, Ricoeur says. In this intimacy there is giving and receiving. This does not mean that the one gives and the other receives, but that both give and both receive, as Ricoeur shows in his analysis of sympathy. What t-akes place in sympathy, not being sympathy as pity, but sympathy as sym-pathy, which -in Greek sun-patheinmeans suffering together? The one person gives his care and love to the other person, who is affected by pain and suffering. The other person receives this care and love. At the same time the first person is reminded by the vulnerability of the person whom he loves, of his own vulnerability, his own passibility and his own mortality. He receives, as it were, his own fragility, his own woundedness. The other person gives that to him. Then, Ricoeur says, the shared whisper of voices takes place or the feeble embrace of clasped hands.

---

2. Küng clearly expresses himself in the epilogue: 'Ja zum ewigen Leben' (p. 283).
3. There is a plurality of opinions and convictions between and within both hermeneutical theologians (cf. Van den Hoogen 1985), like for instance Rahner (1958; 1976), Schillebeeckx (1969; 1989), Kuitert (1992) and analytical anglo-saxian theologians (cf. Mertens 1981; Hick 1989).

Intimacy is born (Ricoeur 1992, 191).[4]

This intimacy analysis gives a foundation to the idea that is expressed by Augustine and more recently by Gabriel Marcel: the vulnerability, the suffering, and the death of the significant other, the intimate friend, are more impressive and affecting than the awareness of one's own finitude, one's own death. Or even better: they evoke the awareness of one's own finitude, one's own death (cf. Ter Borg 1993, 23).

The aspiration, the desire, the longing for life after death emerges at the crossroads of three lines: intimacy (Ricoeur 1992), contingency (Van der Ven 1991), and time, including future (Rahner 1976, 415). In intimacy contingency is experienced: the human passibility and finitude.[5] This contingency stretches out across time, from the past and the present into the future. In that the question emerges: what does the future hold? Is this the end for you and me? Or is there life for you and me beyond death?.[6]

My conclusion is clear. Cutting away these questions from the heart of the Christian faith would imply mutilating the humanity of the Christian faith. Stopping these questions from being placed within the perspective of God's fidelity beyond death would imply amputating the gospel. In other words: death is not merely one of the many themes in the Christian faith, but an exemplary one.

2. Death in Religious Socialization

As I said, we conducted a research project among students of the Catholic University Nijmegen in 1990. This project referred to the students' attitudes with regard to the religious meaning of death. In total, an aselect sample of 637 students,[7] filled in a complete list of items, which were related to seven thanatological attitudes.[8] First, I will describe these attitudes (2.1.). After

---

4.   Cf. the analysis of the solitude of dying by Elias (1982).
5.   According to Vroom (1988, 249), finitude is a basic experience of religion.
6.   According to Schillebeeckx (1977, 249), the idea of life after death is typically religious in nature.
7.   Regarding gender and the first year of registration the sample was representative to the whole student population. The alpha- and betha-students were a bit overrepresented in the sample and the gamma-student a bit underrepresented, as it was also the case with the church going students over against the 'unchurched' (cf. Van der Ven/Biemans 1994).
8.   Four attitudes in the list of seven thanatological attitudes stem from the empirical-theological research by Van Knippenberg (1987; 1988): the teleological, interdependence, contrast and 'aporia' attitudes. However, I labeled the last three of these in a different way: in stead of 'interdependence', 'contrast' and 'aporia', I named them 'interaction', 'intervention' and 'rising,. In this project, the formulation of some items,

that, I will pay attention to the students' thanatological preferences (2.2.).

2.1. Thanatological attitudes

Before going into detail with regard to the content of the thanatological attitudes, I have to clarify what concept of attitude I am referring to. The term attitude can imply very different meanings. Some authors are of the opinion that the term relates to more or less superficial, collective representations of all kinds of aspects of reality, which can easily change over a short period of time. Others think that attitudes are never changing, deeply lying orientations within the emotional infrastructure of the individual's personality, which have been build up in the first decades of his or her life. The first meaning can be found in many sociological studies, whereas the second one is representative for psychodynamic depth-psychology. In this paper, I will take a position in between. For that, I borrow from Fishbein and Azjen (1975) the insight that attitudes imply two different dimensions: a cognitive and an affective one. The cognitive dimension refers to the extent to which the attitudinal topic under consideration is experienced in terms of relevance, usefulness, instrumentality in relation to some life goals of the person involved. It implies the expectation of the extent to which the attitudinal topic contributes to reaching the life goals concerned. The affective dimension refers to the valuing of the life goals themselves, which are connected with the attitudinal topic.

From that insight, the measuring of attitudes has to take into account the two dimensions, which are implied in the attitudes: a cognitive and an affective dimension. The socalled Likert scale may be seen as a way of operationalizing the concept of Azjen and Fishbein. It contains the formulation of a conviction about a certain aspect of reality, that can be seen as relevant or instrumental for one's life goals. At the same time, it contains the formulation of a measure, with the help of which the respondent is able to indicate the value of that aspect of reality, that is implied in the life goals concerned (Jaspars 1981; Swanborn 1982).

Turning now to the thanatological attitudes, I will present them from their cognitive core, because their content and formulation differ, whereas the formulation of the affective dimension, which is based on a five point scale, is always the same (from 'strongly convinced' to 'totally not convinced').

I will present an example of each attitude from its cognitive core and indicate from which theoretical or empirical tradition that example stems. In connection with that, a warning has to be formulated. When a name of a

---

which refer to the four attitudes mentionned, differs from that in Van Knippenberg's study (cf. Van der Ven/Biemans 1994).

specific theologian in relation to a specific attitude is called, for instance Karl Rahner's, the meaning of that reference is not saying that this attitude is at the core of Rahner's personal orientation or of his theological work. The only aim is clarifying in whose work this attitude can be found in the midst of other attitudes.

In order not to be misunderstood by theological readers, I wish to mention that, in the questionnaire, each attitude, which cognitive core will be presented below, was measured by a number of specific items, in the case of the first four theological attitudes by four items each. This means, that the measuring of the theological-thanatological attitudes concerned did not exclusively depend on only one or two items.

The seven thanatological attitudes were: the teleological, interaction, intervention, rising, deism, agnosticism, and immanentism attitude.[9] We added only one item about reincarnation.

The teleological attitude: 'At the moment of death people come to a final decision before God' (Rahner).

The interaction attitude: 'Being aware of daily dying, people may know of eternal living with God' (Tillich).

The intervention attitude: 'After death God creates a new beginning for people' (Jüngel).

The rising attitude: 'Faith in resurrection realizes itself in concrete rising against injustice' (Sölle).

The deism attitude: 'Death is the passage to another existence, whatever that may be' (Felling et al. 1987).

The agnosticism attitude: 'There is much talking about death but I really don't know what to do with it' (Felling et al. 1987).

The immanentism attitude: 'If you have lived your life, death is a natural

---

9.   I will present the formulation of those items which had the highest factor loading within the attitude concerned, except with regard to the teleological attitude, because it has been eliminated from the factor analysis, and except, also, with regard to the interaction and intervention attitude, because both appeared to form only one factor. For that reason, I will present those items concerning the interaction and intervention attitudes, that had the highest average score.

resting-point' (Felling et al. 1987).

The reincarnation attitude, which was formulated from the perspective of popular religion: 'I believe in reincarnation after death' (Thung et al.).

We applied a factor analysis on the items of these attitudes (except the reincarnation item) in order to see which of them would group together from an empirical point of view. I will not deal with technical-statistical details here. I will only pay attention to some interesting points.

At the beginning the factor analysis' output was unclear. That was due to the teleological items. Only 6% of the students or even less agreed with the conviction, that reads: 'At the moment of death people come to a final decision before God'. A minority had doubts about this conviction and a vast majority rejected it. As I said, this teleological attitude stemmed from Rahner (1958). It was already strongly rejected by Schillebeeckx (1970) on the basis of a phenomenological analysis of dying and death, although Schillebeeckx did not explicitly refer to Rahner. Our research showed that Schillebeeckx was right to fight against Rahner's idea. The output with regard to the teleological attitude offers an empirical support to his phenomenological analysis. We decided to eliminate the teleological items on statistical grounds.

After we removed the teleological items the factor analysis could adequately be conducted. Five factors were drawn from a forced five factor solution with the principal axis factoring extraction techniqe, that satisfied the conventional statistical criteria (Van der Ven 1993, 146).

Table 1 – Factor Analysis thanatological attitudes

Theoretical domain:Teleological: b, l, w, ee
       interdependence: c, i, p, bb
       intervention: f, n, u, aa
       rising: e, k, o, t
       deistic: j, q, dd
       theistic: z
       immanentistic: v, y
       agnostic: a, m
       nihilistic: d, g
       reincarnation: s

Empirical domain:christian: c, f, i, n, p, u, z, aa, bb
       deistic: d, j, q, dd
       agnostic: a, m

immanentistic: v, y
rising: k, o, t

item	communality	factor 1	factor 2	factor 3	factor 4	factor 5
u	.89	.99				
aa	.84	.89				
n	.74	.86				
f	.81	.80				
z	.84	.70				
i	.74	.59				
bb	.76	.57				
p	.76	.54				
c	.55	.46				
dd	.73		-.87			
q	.83		-.85			
d	.69		.71			
f	.65		-.69			
m	.75			.85		
a	.26			.51		
v	.47				.68	
y	.25				.45	
t	.64					-.75
o	.57					-.49
k	.49					-.48

total r^2 = 66.3%

The first factor entailed a combination of Tillich's interaction and Jüngel's intervention items. The most important item of the interaction attitude reads: 'Being aware of daily dying people may know of eternal living with God'. The most important item of the intervention attitude reads: 'After death God creates a new beginning for people'. Now, the items of the interaction attitude and of the intervention attitude appeared to form only one factor.[10]

---

10. This happened in both the free four factor solution and the forced five factor solution. The last one we used here.

What does that mean? The students did not distinguish between Tillich's interaction theology and Jüngel's intervention theology. With that, they ran counter to the latest document of the international theological commission, that was published because of Cardinal Ratzinger's instruction in 1992. This document rejected the belief that life after death is to be understood in terms of God's intervention as a new creation, by which, at the moment of death itself, the dead is given new life, without any delay. This conviction denies the so-called two stages eschatology and does not have any place for the im-mortality of the soul (Internationale theologische commissie 1992). But for the students, this two stages eschatology and all the details implied in it, is irrelevant. For them, there is only one insight, that is implied in both Tillich's and Jüngel's interpretation, namely that people live in God after death. The students favour the common core of Tillich and Jüngel. They totally transcend their differences. I labelled this factor 'Christian faith in life after death'. I did that from the insight that the specific religious interpretati-on of death within the Christian faith says: 'living with God is stronger than the death', and 'there is, beyond death, a real communion with God and because of that also with people ('communio sanctorum'), in a totally different way – what ever the specific concretization of this new life may be' (Schillebeeckx 1977, 737).

The second factor existed of three items, which referred to Sölle's rising attitude. It is remarkable that it formed an isolated factor, separately from the interaction and the intervention attitude, or, better, separately from the factor 'Christian faith in life after death'. In Van Knippenberg's study also, this factor plaid a special role (Van Knippenberg 1987, 126-130, 208-209). The question may be asked, whether the students did not recognize or accept the Christian loading of Sölle's and other theologians' societal criticism with regard to death?

The third factor contained four items, which related to what I earlier called 'deism'. It is interesting that it separated itself from both 'the christian faith in life after death' and 'the rising attitude'. The vague, general-transcendental meaning, that the students attributed to death, did not fit, at least from their perspective, into the classical-Christian and the society-critical interpretation.

The fourth factor entailed two items, that were labelled as 'agnosticism'. The factor-analytical separation between 'deism' and 'agnosticism is relevant indeed. Having a vague, general-transcendental notion about life after death appeared to be different from having no idea at all.

The fifth factor existed of two items, that were called 'immanentism'. Again, a vague, general-transcendental notion, agnosticism and immanentism are really different, from the students' consciousness. Immanentism says that death is the ultimate end of life. There is no other perspective, no other possibility even.

As I said, we added only one item about reincarnation: 'I believe in reincarnation after death'. This item was stripped of its explicit Hindu and Buddhist connotations .[11] and was formulated from the frame of reference of popular religion (Hick 1989, 367-368). We did not put that item in our factor analysis. Nevertheless, in the following, I will deal with it, because it will appear to throw an interesting light on our findings.

2.2. Thanatological preferences

Which average values did the students attribute to the thanatological attitudes? A question that I would like to add, is: did it make a difference if students defined themselves as religious or non-religious? Did the religious students score higher or lower than the non-religious ones? About 55% of the students of the Catholic University at Nijmegen defined themselves as religious and about 45% as non-religious.[12]

In table 2 the first column refers to the total population, the second to the religious subpopulation, and the third to the non-religious subpopulation. The numbers in these columns may vary from 1 ('I totally disagree') to 5 ('I totally agree'). The numbers in the fourth column refer to the extent to which the differences between the religious and the nonreligious students are statistically significant, that means whether they are based on chance or not, which is indicated by the so-called 'eta'. Only the eta's which are not based on chance (which are thus significant), are mentioned in the fourth column. The higher the eta, which can run from .00 to 1.00, the stronger the difference between the religious and the non-religious subpopulation.

---

11. Within the Hindu tradition, a number of different conceptions of reincarnation can be distinguished, which refer to different relationships between dharma, karma and moksja (Vroom 1988, 87-89). For the Buddhist commotations see for example: Rahula 1982, 31-34.

12. In 1988/1989 a survey was conducted among a sample of 703 protestant students in Germany, from which 41% of them appeared to define themselves as religious and 34% as non-religious, whereas 25% indicated not having decided jet (Ahrens/Schloz 1992, 16).

Table 2 – Mean scores thanatological attitudes

	total	religious	non-religious	eta
chr.life after death	2.3	2.9	1.7	.58
rising	2.4	2.8	1.9	.47
deism	3.1	3.6	2.4	.58
agnosticism	2.9	2.9	2.9	n.s.
immanentism	3.6	3.5	3.7	.15
reincarnation	2.4	2.7	2.1	.24

range: 1 (totally disagree) to 5 (totally agree)

Let us begin with the first column that refers to the total population. Only one attitude was positive in character, because it found itself on the right half of the middle of the scale (3.00): immanentism (3.6). All students agreed that death is the natural resting-point of life. What appears from the second column? The religious students attributed the highest value to deism (3.6) and again to immanentism (3.5). The Christian convictions of life after death and of rising were stuck beneath the middle of the scale (2.9, 2.8). This also applied to agnosticism (2.9). In the third column the non-religious students systematically scored lower with regard to the Christian faith of life after death (1.7), and of rising (1.9), and with regard to deism (2.4). They systematically scored higher with regard to immanentism (3.7). There was only one exception: The religious and non-religious students did not show any difference with regard to agnosticism (2.9).

I did not speak about reincarnation yet. The religious students scored significantly higher than the non-religious students (2.7, 2.1). From table 3, 21% of the religious students appeared to believe in reincarnation and only 9% of the non-religious students.

Table 3 – Reincarnation attitudes in %

	total	religious	non-religious
totally disagree	26.3	18.5	36.1
disagree	24.7	24.8	24.7
disagree\agree	33.3	35.7	30.2
agree	10.3	12.5	7.5
totally agree	5.4	8.5	1.6

Cramers' V = .24   p < .05

The belief in reincarnation appeared to be present especially among the religious and less among the non-religious subpopulation (Cramers' V = 24). From table 4, the correlation coefficient between the belief in reincarnation and deism (.51) transcended the coefficients with the Christian faith in life after death (.19), rising (.33) and agnosticism (.15).

Table 4 – Reincarnation and thanatological attitudes (Pearson r)

	Christian faith	Rising	Deism	Agnosticism	Imanentism
reincar-ation	.19	.31	.51	.15	n.s.

$p < .05$

In other words, the conviction of reincarnation can not be set aside, as if it were a non-religious phenomenon. In more general terms, these data support Schillebeeckx' insight that faith in life after death, in any formulation what so ever, has a religious loading (Schillebeeckx 1977, 736).

Nevertheless, from the tables, which were presented above, the general conclusion can be drawn that the socialization with regard to the religious interpretation of death has been ineffective, at least from the perspective of the Christian religion. Even among the religious students both Christian convictions that we measured -life after death and rising- run counter to doubt. The only two convictions, with which the religious students agree, are deistic belief and immanentism.[13]

3. Factors in Religious Socialization about Death

Now we ask the question which factors in religious socialization influenced the students' attitudes with regard to the religious interpretation of death. First, I will pay attention to the question, which factors have to be dealt with (3.1.). After that, I ask the question what the real influence of these factors was (3.2.).

3.1. The choice of factors
Which factors might be of importance here? Answering this question implies

---

13. On a five point scale, the scores between 1.00 and 1.80 indicate total rejection, between 1.81 and 2.60 rejection, between 2.61 and 3.40 doubt, between 3.41 and 4.20 agreement, and between 4.21 and 5.00 total agreement.

a theory about socialization, viz. religious socialization. But, I do not wish to present a number of different psychological and sociological socialization theories, from which the factors to be selected could be legitimized. These theories vary from depth-psychological to social-psychological to functionalistic and society-critical sociological approaches. I would like to restrict myself in a pragmatic way to mentioning four factors, which are, in my opinion, relevant for the question under consideration in this paper. These factors are: mimesis, family education, school education and knowledge development.

I restrict mimesis to practical mimesis, as this is elaborated on by Bourdieu following Plato. Practical mimesis is imitating other people, but without being explicitly aware of it. With regard to practical mimesis I assume that children unreflectively copy their father's and mother's faith. I suppose that children automatically attribute the same saliency to the Christian faith, as they see their father and mother do. I presuppose that children participate in ecclesial life in the same way as their father and mother do, without being conscious of it, up to a certain age (cf. Van de Slik 1992, 143). From a cognitive, social-psychological perspective this practical mimesis can be labelled as 'observational learning' (Bandura 1986, 47ff.).

I make a distinction between mimesis and family education. Mimesis takes place in the family, especially, by which the parents and the children interact with each other and participate in each others' world without having the intention to do so, or without, even, knowing it. One might call it -to use a fundamental concept from pedagogics- 'informal education'. This 'informal education' has to be distinguished -according to this fundamental-pedagogical thinking- from 'intentional education'. Within 'intentional education', the educators are consciously aiming at reaching certain educational effects, viz. cognitive, emotional, attitudinal or behavioral effects (cf. Meijer 1992, 24). In this paper, I call this 'intentional education' shortly 'education'. In that, I distinguish between the following elements: religious communication which exists in a shared reading of the bible and the telling of religious stories; further religious transfer, whereby the parents express their concern about the child taking over specific convictions and values; lastly religious steering, whereby the parents impose certain obligations, as for example going to church.

Religious education in the family and in the school are two different things. I distinguish between participating in a confessional, Christian, private school on the one hand and getting religious education in terms of religious instruction or catechetics on the other.

Lastly, I mention developing religious knowledge. This development takes place within both the family and the school, whereas it also realizes itself outside of it, for example within the frame of reference of the mass media. We measured religious knowledge with regard to stories and figures from the

Old Testament, the New Testament, liturgy and today's ecclesial praxis.[14]

3.2. Influencing factors

Let's have a look at table 5. The vertical axis refers to the factors in religious socialization just mentioned. They divided into four groups: mimesis, family, school, and religious knowledge. The horizontal axis relates to the thanatological attitudes, viz. the Christian faith in life after death, in rising, deism, agnosticism, immanentism, and reincarnation. The numbers in the table are eta coefficients, which can run from .00 to 1.00.

Table 5 – Factors in religious socialization (eta)

	chr.after death	rising	deism	agnost.	imman.	reincarn.
mimesis						
faith father	.35	.30	.26	–	–	–
faith mother	.42	.30	.31	–	–	–
sal. father	.38	.32	.24	–	–	–
sal. mother	.41	.31	.28	–	–	–
church father	.34	.31	.21	–	–	–
church mother	.36	.29	.20	–	–	–
family						
relig.comm.	.32	.27	.22	–	–	–
relig.transfer	.39	.28	.20	–	–	–
relig.steering	.19	.17	–	–	–	–
school						
public/confess	.20	.18	–	–	–	–
religious educ.	–	–	–	–	–	–
relig.knowledge	.40	.36	–	–	–	–

$p < .05$

---

14. In the Dutch newspapers of l0th April 1993, Easter saturday, one could read the results of an investigation, saying that more than the half of the Dutch population did not know the meaning of 'Easter' any longer. This did not apply to the Nijmegen students. To mention some findings: 88% knew what 'Advent' is, 77% what is the name of Sunday before Easter, and 73% what the meaning of Holy Thursday is. Evidently, one might say that 12%, 23%, and 27% did not know it!

What does the table show? Let me first pay attention to the left half of the table. This half refers to three thanatological attitudes: the Christian attitude referring to life after death, to rising, and the deistic attitude. These attitudes were strongly influenced by religious mimesis and – within family education – by religious communication and religious transfer. This especially applied to the Christian convictions of life after death and of rising, and a bit less to the deistic faith in life after death. Religious steering in family education (sending children to church) and participating in confessional schools did not appear to influence the religious attitudes so much. Catechetics in schools had no influence at all. It is very remarkable that developing religious knowledge, that can be seen as the common result of religious education in the family and in the school, dominantly influenced the faith in life after death and in rising (.40. and .36). The transfer of religious knowledge is important. With that, I do not plea for a universal, world catechism catechetics, but for a solid form of transferring modern religious knowledge.[15]

Let us turn now to the right half of the table. This half refers to agnosticism, immanentism and reincarnation. No significant or relevant influence[16] could be observed between mimesis, family education, school education and religious knowledge on the one hand and agnosticism, immanentism and reincarnation on the other. The belief in reincarnation found itself in a special position, because, unlike agnosticism and immanentism, which have their roots in the Enlightenment, it is a relatively recent phenomenon, so that it could not have been socialized to the students yet.

In other words, how ever religious parents may be, how ever salient religion may be for them, how ever intensely they participate in ecclesial life, how ever frequently they discuss religious themes with their children, how ever concerned they may be in transferring religious values, how ever steering they may be, how ever much they want their children to go to confessional schools and receive knowledge-based religious instruction: all this does not influence the extent to which their children show an agnostic, an immanentistic, or a reincarnation oriented attitude at all.

4. Consequences for Ecclesial and Pastoral Policy

The empirical results that I presented with the help of the tables 4 and 5, can

---

15. From the historical research, that I conducted many years ago, I rejected any form of world catechism catechetics, as I also rejected the desirability and achievability of the returning idea of a world catechism itself (Van der Ven 1976; 1985, 206-208; cf. Bulckens 1994).

16. The significance criterium is $p < .05$, and the relevance criterium is eta $> .15$.

be reflected upon from different insights. I will treat them from the perspectives of the family (4.1.), the school (4.2.), the cultural decor (4.3.), and the mass media (4.4.).

4.1. The family

The first perspective refers to the family. On the one hand the family is important for transferring Christian and religious convictions with regard to life after death. It evidently influences the Christian faith in life after death, the faith in rising and the deistic awareness. Especially mimesis, the unconscious imitation behaviour by children in correspondence with that of the parents, is important. At this point, our research supports the conclusion from Dutch research about religious socialization of youngsters in general (De Hart 1990, 183). But religious communication and religious transfer, which take place in the family, also influence youth' religious attitudes, as our research showed. At this point too, our project supports the findings of religious socialization research in general (De Hart 1990, 177-181).

On the other hand, the danger of exaggerating the family's role really exists. I would like to point at two different phenomena, which are implied in the tables.

The first refers to the high eta coefficients between mimesis and family education on the one hand and the Christian faith in life after death, in rising and deism. What do these high coefficients really mean? They indicate that students, to the extent to which they were brought up in really Christian families, show, now, religious attitudes. But, the reverse is also true: the students show non-religious orientations, to the extent to which they were educated in non-religious families. To say this in a different way: the eta coefficients indicate the association not only between religious upbringing and actual religious attitudes, but also between non-religious upbringing and actual non-religious attitudes. The conclusion should be: Dutch families are experts in both religious and non-religious socialization! But at the same time, they can be used for preventing asking some specific questions. One question is, how many students had a religious family education and how many had not, how many students now define themselves as religious and how many do not. Now, more than 50 % of the students call themselves religious, only more than 40 % Christian, and only nearly 20 % ecclesially engaged. That is much less than the high eta coefficients might suggest! Another question is, how many students who received a really religious upbringing, went their own way, and distanciated themselves from the Christian faith later on. To give some indications: from the students who participated in an outspoken form of religious communication within their parental families, more than 20 % does not belief in God or has difficulties with it, and 10 % has doubts about it, whereas two third beliefs more or less in Him. To give another example: from the students who received a well-intended and convincing transfer of religious values by their parents, more than 15% has distanciated them selves more or less from the belief in God, nearly 10% has doubts about it, whereas nearly 75% beliefs more or less in Him (Van der Ven/Biemans 1994). In other words, besides the coefficients, we always need the classic cross tables in order to see what is really going on (Janssen 1988; De Hart 1990, 140; 1990a, 64-66)!

The second phenomenon that I would like to refer to, relates to the data with regard to the attitudes of agnosticism, immanentism, and reincarnation. These attitudes appear to develop separately from processes taking place in the family. I point at the fact that both religious and non-religious students totally agree with immanentism. The family does not influence the immanent attitude, neither in a positive nor in a negative way. Its influence is null and void. From this point of view, exaggerated ideas, that people sometimes entertain with regard to the family, have to be relativized. An exaggerated opinion can be found, for example, in the document of the Roman Catholic National Pastoral Consultation in the Netherlands ('Landelijk Pastoraal Overleg'), of which the title is 'Catechetics and Parish' ('Katechese en Parochie'). I quote: 'Almost all investigations of recent years say that the influence of the parents is the main factor that advances the youngsters' religious education -and now the reader's critical attention is required – against societal pressure' (Informatiebullet 1992, 6, 24). It is right to say that the influence of the parents is the main factor, but not against societal pressure! I would like to distance myself from Kaufmann's thesis that the role of the family could nearly be overestimated (Kaufmann 1979, 186). To my opinion, the family is more overestimated than underestimated, as it appears to be the case in the official statement of Cardinal Danneels saying that family pastoral care is and should be one of the main objectives of pastoral policy (Danneels 1993, 34).

4.2. The school

The second perspective from which the empirical results can be reflected upon, refers to the school. Whereas the family is mostly overestimated in ecclesial and pastoral policy, the school is often underestimated. Nevertheless, participating in confessional schools appears to contribute to religious socialization with regard to the Christian interpretation of death. Religious instruction at school appears to be neglectable. But, if religious instruction is connected with developing religious knowledge, it could be very influential. With that I am entering upon a battle field. The battle that has already been going for about 30 years, refers to the question: what is the relevance of developing religious knowledge for developing religious attitudes? The protagonists of the universal catechism catechetics stress the importance of religious knowledge. The antagonists, who pay a lot of attention to the attitudinal development of pupils and students, interpret stressing developing religious knowledge in terms of an evil that has to be fight against and removed. But, for theoretical and empirical reasons I am of the opinion that this fight is fruitless and perspectiveless. Why? To put it in only one principle: which ever religious attitudes have to be developed, whether they be conservative or progressive, they both need the development of religious knowledge: conservative religious knowledge for conservative attitudes, progressive religious knowledge for progressive attitudes. In order not be misunderstood: developing religious knowledge is a necessary condition for developing religious attitudes, not a sufficient one. This means: without developing religious knowledge, developing religious attitudes is an illusion. But, at the same time one should say: developing religious attitudes can not be reduced to developing religious knowledge. The most important reason why this reduction is not legitimate, is implied in the influence that is exerted by the social environment. The social environment is necessary for upholding and reinforcing the individual's attitude. If one's own attitude runs into the conventional (religious or non-religious) attitudes of one's social environment, the chance that this attitude will survive, is relatively small. For that reason, developing religious attitudes depend on at least two main factors: cognitive and social ones. The empirical basis of this principle is implied in interpreting developing attitudes in general in terms of an information and communication process in a social context (Jaspars 1981; Huismans 1984). My question is whether the evident neglection of religious knowledge during the last 30 years -a period of time that spans a whole generation- strongly contributed to the partial ineffectiveness of religious socialization.

4.3. The cultural decor

The third perspective from which the empirical data can be reflected upon, refers to the cultural decor (Van de Slik 1992, 141), against the background of which religious socialization in the family and the school takes place. It relates to the cultural space outside the family and the school. We saw that developing attitudes of agnosticism, immanentism and reincarnation transcended the influence of the family and the school. Religious socialization is not only the result of education, but also of effects that go beyond the family and the school. Here, I mention three of them: the other socialization effects, period effects, and generation effects.

First, the other socialization effects refer to the influences, that stem from, for example, peer groups, associations, and mass media. The peer groups and associations may send messages that correspond to those that are sent in religious education in the family and the school, but they also may neutralize them or even hinder them and work against them (Vervoort 1975, 72-73). The mass media, for example, have an anything but friendly approach with regard to religion (Henau 1992; 1993).

Second, the period effects have to be understood as the effects of the 'Zeitgeist', the social-economic and cultural climate. From this perspective, the sixties and the seventies are labelled as the period of the cultural revolution, whereas the eighties are called that of no-nonsense. This whole time is characterized by the processes of individualization and secularization (Peters 1993). These processes take place in a

cultural environment, almost totally independent from the individual's freedom, choice and decision. Cultural processes sometimes look like meterological phenomena: it is difficult to forecast them, and when they take place, they condition or even determine almost everything in life! The period effects on religious socialization are not easily overestimated.

Lastly, the generation effects also influence religious socialization. Research shows, for instance, that the whole generation that has been born since 1955, believes significantly less in a personal than in a non-personal God, if it beliefs in God what so ever, whereas the previous generations placed their trust in a personal God (Van Dam 1992, 73-74).

In other words, religious education in the family and the school is not a match for the other socialization effects, the period and the generation effects.

4.4. The mass media

The question becomes urgent: how should ecclesial and pastoral policy be developed? This is the fourth perspective from which the data can be reflected upon. My answer is: positively valuing and stimulating both the family and the school and within that developing religious knowledge. Next to that, anything else still has to be done. The church should actively use the cultural space outside the family and the school in order to develop religious communication. Let me take the mass media as an example, in order to formulate some thoughts with regard to (A) the goal, (B) the target groups and (C) the method of religious communication.

A. The goal of this religious communication should not be fighting internal-theological and internal-ecclesial battles about this or that interpretation of themes within the Christian faith. Those internal fights transcend the average student. As our research showed, the models of such conflicting theological schools like those of Tillich and Jüngel appeared to form one factor. The average student does not have a consciousness structure that has any room for these internal battles. Not the one or two stage eschatology does interest him or her, but the eschatological hope itself: whether there is some perspective of living with God after death! The real struggle is not about internal disputes, but about something different, namely: the gap between the Christian and religious interpretation of life and death on the one hand and agnostic and immanentistic interpretations on the other. The real discussion is about transcendence and immanence. Religious communication should first and foremost orient itself to the gap between transcendence and immanence. From this point of view, TV-discussions about ecclesial power processes are counter-productive. The same applies to broadcasting conflicts between church leaders and theologians or between theologians among each other about encyclics, like 'Humanae vitae' or 'Splendor veritatis'. They are ineffective, to say the least.

B. The target groups for whom the struggle between transcendence and immanence has to be fought, are not only non-religious people. Religious, even Christian, or even church-going people are at least as important. Immanentism is not only positively valued by the non-religious students, as our research showed, but also by the religious students, and even the Christian and the church-going students. Not only nonreligious students, but also religious, Christian and churchgoing students appeared to have problems with transcendence over against immanence. As our research showed, the religious, Christian and church-going students had a positive attitude with regard to immanentism (resp. 3.5, 3.5 and 3.4), whereas the religious students were characterized by a negative doubt with regard to the Christian faith in life after death, and the Christian and Church-going student by a positive doubt (resp. 2.9, 3.1 and 3.3). Not by a positive attitude! One might even say: to the extent that the students are more religious, more Christian, or even more church-oriented, the dilemma 'transcendence versus immanence' becomes sharper and sharper. Dilemmas are inherent in any world view, like for instance the dilemmas between freedom and equality, freedom and authority, equality and authority (Billing et al. 1988). Because dilemmas are dilemmas, they evoke cognitive and emotional ambivalence and ambiguity (Billing 1982, 167-202; Van der Lans 1991). For that reason they require recognition instead of repression and suppression, clarification instead of tabooing, a dialogue in stead of a monologue. This also applies to the dilemma between transcendence and immanence within the domain of religious world views, especially the Christian faith.

C. Lastly, I would like to formulate some suggestions about the method of religious communication. From the data, the Christian interpretation of life after death appears to be the conviction of a social and cognitive minority. Only the Christian students (43%) and the church-going students

(19%) find themselves on the positive side of the scale, although they have some doubts about it (3.1., 3.3.). With that they run counter to the majority of the students. They criticize, as it were, the general plausibility of the world view of immanentism, with which they even identify themselves, as we saw! They show deviant behaviour, about which they strongly feel ambivalent emotions.

From research we know how people behave, if they form a minority, that runs counter to the majority's convictions and values. They legitimate their deviant ideas and actions by giving reasons for it by telling stories. They tell stories about concrete incidents about concrete persons in concrete situations, from which the generally plausible world view appears not to work and why they distanced themselves from this world view. Because of the drama in those stories and because of the plot in those stories, a rhetorical situation emerges, that enables those deviant people to convince the others, or at least to strive for convincing the others (Bruner 1990). If afterwards they are asked to give further explanation, then they try to take into account the majority's convictions as much as possible in their own comment and to relate their own convictions to them. With that, they are aiming, from a rhetorical perspective, at winning the others for their own points of view, their own conviction, beliefs, and values (Lemmens 1993).[17] That means: they exchange perspectives. So, two things are important: both story telling and exchanging perspectives. If the acting of ecclesial authorities at home and abroad is compared with story-telling and perspective exchanging minorities, a sharp difference comes to the fore. He who does not function narratively and does not explain the narrations in a rhetoric-narrative mode, but starts his proclamation with phrases like 'the church teaches us' or even worse 'the church teaches us, it can not be altered' does not have in mind the fact that he belongs to a social and cognitive minority. From rhetoric research the plea should be formulated, at least in my view, to replace dogmatics by narratives, kerugma by drama, authoritatives by communicatives, commissives by suggestives, eternal worlds by possible worlds, truth claims by historical guesses, perspective posing by perspective exchanging, closed mindedness by open-mindedness. In a culture, in which the Christian faith is based on a social and cognitive minority, religious socialization requires such policy change. Without such a change religious socialization about death will come to a dead end.

---

17. Here, in rhetorical terms, rhetorical concessions are at stake, which refer to taking up discongruent arguments into one's own discourse. The question, whether one succeeds in that, evidently depends on the extent to which one is emotionally involved in the theme under consideration.

Literature

Ahrens P.A., Schloz R. (1992). Protestant Students in Germany, in: Journ. of Emp. Theol. 5 (1992) 2, 5 – 30

Aristoteles. Ethica Nicomacheia.

Bandura A. (1986). Social Foundations of Thought and Action. Englewood Cliffs.

Billig M. (1982). Ideology and Social Psychology. Oxford.

Billig M. et al. (1988). Ideological Dilemmas. A Social Psychology of Every Day Thinking. London.

Blenkinsopp J. (1970). Theologische synthese en hermeneutische conclusies. In: Concilium 6 (1970) 10, 111 – 123

Borg M. ter (1993). De dood als het einde. Een cultuur-sociologisch essay. Baarn

Bruner J. (1990). Acts of meaning. Cambridge, Massachusetts.

Bulckens J. (1994). Catechese, catechismus en opbouw van een milieu van geloof. In: J.A. van der Ven, A. Houtepen (red.), Weg van de kerk. Reflecties op 'De pastorale arbeid in de negentiger jaren' van bisschop Ernst. Kampen.

Dam B. van (1992). Een generatie met verschillende gezichten, Culturele diversiteit onder de jonge volwassene van de jaren tachtig. diss. KUN, ITS, Nijmegen.

Danneels G. (1993). Toespraak tot Paus Johannes Paulus II bij gelegenheid van het Ad Limina-bezoek van de Belgische bisschoppen in juli 1992. In: Kerkelijke documentatie 1-2-1 21(1993)1, 33-36

Elias N. (1982). Über die Einsamkeit der Sterbenden. Frankfurt.

Felling A., Peters J., Schreuder O. (1987). Religion in Dutch Society. Steinmetz Archive. Amsterdam.

Fishbein M., Ajzen I. (1975). Belief, Attitude, Intention and Behaviour. An Introduction to Theory and Research. New York.

Hart J. de (1990). Impact of Religious Socialization in the Family. In: Journ. of Emp. Theol. 3(1990)1, 59-78

Hart J. de (1990). Levensbeschouwelijke en politieke praktijken van Nederlandse middelbare scholieren. Kampen.

Henau E. (1992). Theological Reflection on Gibson's article. In: Journ. of Emp. Theol. 5(1992)1, 31-32

Henau E. (1993). God op de buis. Leuven.

Hick J. (1989). An Interpretation of Religion. Human Responses to the Transcendent. New Haven.

Hoogen T. van den (1985). De liefde en de dood. Een peiling naar de actuele discussie over eschatologie. In: Tijds.v.Theol. 25(1985)3, 278-298

Huismans S. E. (1984). Attitudeverandering in de praktijk. In: Jaspars J., Vlist R. van der. Sociale psychologie in Nederland, I. Deventer, 193-234

Internationale theologische commissie (1992). Enkele actuele onderwerpen over de eschatologie. In: Kerkelijke documentatie 1-2-1 20(1992) 4, 21-50

Janssen J. (1988) De jeugd, de toekomst en de religie. In: Jeugd en samenleving 18(1988)7/8, 422vv.

Jaspars J., Vlist R. van der (1979). Sociale psychologie in Nederland, I-IV. Deventer.

Jüngel E. (1976). Der Tod als Geheimnis des Lebens. In: Schwartländer J. (Hrsg.). Der Mensch und sein Tod (108-125). Tübingen.

Jüngel E. (1977). Gott als Geheimnis der Welt. Tübingen.

Kaufmann F.-X. (1979). Kirche begreifen. Analysen und Thesen zur gesellschaftlichen Verfassung des Christentums. Freiburg.

Knippenberg M. van (1987). Dood en religie. Een studie naar communicatief zelfonderzoek in het pastoraat. Serie Theologie en Empirie, Deel 6. Kampen.

Knippenberg M. van (1988). Communicative Self-Investigation in Pastoral Group work. Journal of Empirical Theology 1(1988)2, 64-88

Küng H. (1982). Ewiges Leben. München.

Kuitert H. (1992). Het algemeen betwijfeld christelijk geloof. Baarn.

Lans J. van der (1991). Culturele ambivalentie en het onderzoek naar wereldbeelden. In: Felling A., Peters J. (red.), Cultuur en sociale wetenschappen. ITS. Nijmegen, 91-106

Lemmens L., Persoonlijke meningen (1993). De invloed van attitudinaal affect, persoonlijke betrokkenheid en sociale context op de structuur van privé-meningsuitingen. Diss. KUN. Nijmegen.

Logister W. (1988). Het terughoudend spreken over verrijzenis in het oude testament. In: Tijds.v.Theol. 28(1988) 1, 3-25

Meijer W.A.J. (1992). Het jonge kind en de cultuur. In: Prakt. Theol. 19(1992), 335-348

Mertens H.-E. (1981). Tendenzen in de engelstalige eschatologie, in: Tijds.v.Theol. 21(1981)4, 407-421

Peters J. (1993). Individualisering en secularisering in Nederland in de jaren tachtig. Sociologie als contemporaine geschiedbeschrijving. ITS. Nijmegen.

Rahula W. (1982). What he Buddha taught. London.

Rahner K. (1958). Zur Theologie des Todes. Freiburg.

Rahner K. (1976). Grundkurs des Glaubens. Einführung in den Begriff des Christentums. Freiburg.

Ricoeur P. (1992). Oneself As Another. Chicago.

Schillebeeckx E. (1969). Enkele hermeneutische beschouwingen over de eschatologie. Concilium 5(1969)1, 38-51.

Schillebeeckx E. (1970). Leven ondanks de dood in heden en toekomst. In: Tijds.v.Theol. 10(1970)4, 418-452

Schillebeeckx E. (1977). Gerechtigheid en liefde, genade en bevrijding. Bloemendaal.

Schillebeeckx E. (1989). Mensen als verhaal van God. Baarn.

Schoonenberg P. (1969). Hij is een God van mensen. Twee theologische studies. Den Bosch.

Slik F. van der (1992). Overtuigingen, attituden, gedrag en ervaringen. Een onderzoek naar de godsdienstigheid van ouders en van hun kinderen. Diss. Theol. Fac. Tilburg. Nijmegen.

Sociaal en Cultureel Rapport 1992 (1992). Sociaal en Cultureel Planbureau. Rijswijk.

Sölle D. (1973). Leiden. (Ned. vert.: Lijden.) Baarn.

Swanborn P.G. (1982). Schaaltechnieken. Meppel.

Tillich P. (1966). Systematic theology I-III. Chicago.

Thung M. e.a. (1985). Exploring the New Religious Consciousness. Amsterdam.

Ven J.A. van der (1976). Katechese en bisschopsambt, Het bisschopsambt (176-201). In: Annalen van het Thijmgenootschap. Ambo. Bilthoven.

Ven J.A. van der (1985). Aspecten van de religieuze ervaring in het perspectief van het cognitief interactionisme. In: J. Bulckens e.a. (red.). Een stap is mij genoeg (pp. 197-214). Amersfoort.

Ven J.A. van der (1991). Religieuze variaties, in: Tijds. v. Theol. 31 (1991)2, 163-182.

Ven J.A. van der (1993). Practical Theology: An Empirical Approach, Kampen 1993.

Ven J.A. van der (1994). Ecclesiology in Context, Eerdmans. Grand Rapids (in print).

Ven J.A. van der, Biemans B. (1994). Religie in fragmenten. Een onderzoek onder studenten. Serie Theologie & Empirie 20. Kok, Kampen/DSV, Weinheim.

Ven J.A. van der, Ziebertz H.-G. (Hrsg.). Paradigmenentwicklung in der Praktischen Theologie, Kok, Kampen/DSV, Weinheim 1993.

Vervoort C. (1975). Onderwijs en maatschappij. Link. Nijmegen.

Vroom H.M. (1988). Religies en de waarheid. Kampen.

VI Religious Socialisation and Shaping a Church Community

A. de Jong

In our western society we tend increasingly to emphasize individual freedom of choice. Self development and individual wellbeing are recognised as an important social value. Often we set personal interest above the interest of society. This structural orientation towards the individual is linked with a lessening social watchfulness. Sociologists call this development 'individualisation'. They become especially aware of this in the fields of religion and morality (Ester a.o. 1993).

Without doubt this phenomenon is an important cause of the decline in church membership in Europe. Under pressure from this individualisation, various social connections have lost their attractiveness. This goes for trade unions and political parties, cultural institutions and sporting clubs. But it is particular true for churches. Especially during the last decades, churches have to face a decreasing membership and less participation. This decline in church membership began early in this century. Since the sixties, however, it has accellerated. At the moment, in the Netherlands, a clear majority of the population no longer considers itself part of a church community. It is thought likely that this trend will continue, and that, by 2020, only one fourth of the Dutch population will consider itself as churchmembers (Becker 1994). This trend is not restricted to the Netherlands. While the Netherlands headed the list of countries where churches were avoided in 1990, during the eighties, the number of people who stayed out of church in Belgium, Great Britain and France has grown to a much higher degree than it has in the Netherlands. Only Germany, where about 90% of the population is formally member of a church community, seems to be an exception. If, however, we look at the degree of involvement in the church, we find that it is much lower than in the Netherlands. In France, the degree of involvement in the church, is still lower (van Hemert, 1994, 25-27). It seems reasonable to assume that the decline in church membership will increase over the whole of Western Europe, unless completely unexpected changes take place.

Both the decline of church membership and the individualisation at its root, impede the religious socialisation within our western society. With this I mean in this context not only the way our young people are spontaneously influenced in a religious socialisation in a narrow sense. I intend to use the term in a broader sense to refer also to an intended religious schooling or a spiritual education within family, school and church. In how far this influence is spontaneous or planned does not matter in this respect. While individualisation and decline of church membership offer new possibilities for religious socialisation, they cause great problems for the religious education. This goes for both forms of religious socialisation.

This context makes a possible contribution by religious socialisation toward shaping a church community particularly difficult. With this I mean all activities which are intended to promote a collective experience of faith within an institutional union. No one can undertake such activities alone. People have to work together. In the old, popular ecclesiastical situation this was a different matter. Then, nearly everyone was a church member, and things ran practically their own course. People seemed to grow into the church automatically. Religious socialisation was practically the same as ecclesiastical socialisation. With the decline of church membership and the increase in individualisation, this has changed completely. Religious socialisation can no longer be a ready made foundation for the formation of a community and for the construction of an ecclastiastical community. On the contrary, religious educationists sometimes speak of religious desocialisation (Mette 1983, 29 etc.). This poses a big problem. For in the long term, faith cannot exist without a church. At a time when church is becoming less and less a matter of course, we have to work harder to build up our ecclesiastical communities, if we want our faith and church to have a future. This is possible only when people are willing and able to accept religious socialisation in a church context.

How can the still existing religious socialisation in this context of individualisation and church neglect, lay a foundation for shaping a church community? This is the question, I attempt to answer in this article. I am concerned less with methodology or the social circles, in which this would be possible, than I am with answers to the question, what are the desirable and possible mental effects of religious socialisation. Which effects, intended or not, permit people to want and be able to participate in activities that shape a church community?

An answer to this question may be expected to be found in the practical theological study of religious education. During the last decades, however, the study of religious education has given little attention to this question. In the second part of this article I intended to explain this further. First, however, I will address the question of where religious education might look for a satisfactory solution to the problem of how religious socialisation can contribute to shaping a church community. In the third part, I shall endeavour to indicate that direction more precisely. With a view to this. I shall first enter into the question of the preconditions for shaping a church community.

1. Shaping Church Community as Collective Behaviour

In this context it seems to me to be obvious that the building up of a church community is a form of collective behaviour. This aspect is often neglected. In a closer analysis of that aspect there lies the key for an answer to the central question of this article. Shaping a church community is, as we know, not a spontaneous process of development, but a matter of purposeful group action. What does this imply? What is the logical structure of such acting? What is needed for people to be able to join in such activities? The answers to these questions may point the way for religious education to a solution to the problem of what has to be done within the religious socialisation to promote the shaping of a church community. For this analysis we use a number of enlightening views on collective behaviour in general put forth by the American philosopher J.R. Searle in his article 'Collective Intentions and Actions' (Searle 1990).

The Nature of Collective Behaviour
Shaping a church community as collective behaviour is a form of intentional activity. When we speak of shaping a church community, we mean activities, behaviour in the same sense of doing things, whereby intentions are being realised. A typifying and distinguishing feature of intentions is, that within this mental representation of the activity concerned, world is linked to mind. The direction of fit here is world-to-mind. In this respect, intentions differ in meaning from perception, memories or religious convictions. In these cognitive forms of intentionality, mind is fitted to the world and the direction of fit is therefore mind-to-world. The direction of fit concerns the question of what causes failures or mistakes. If a (religious) conviction is false somewhere, this is due to the conviction and not to reality. But if an attempt to realise an intention fails, this is not due to the intention but to the action. The direction of fit is not the same as the direction of causation. The direction of causation does not concern the 'success' or the 'failure' of mental representation, but the question whether they are brought about by something else, or bring about something else. Intentions have a direction of causation of mind-to-world, for it is the intention that causes the action. Where convictions, memories or perception are concerned, it is the reverse. These are caused by something within the reality. So they have a direction of causation of world-to-mind. The direction of causation of intentional states appears to be exactly opposed to their direction of fit. In connection with a build-up of a church community this is a crucial fact. For however important (religious) convictions or other 'cognitive' states may be to shaping a church community, it is not in itself made up of intentional states with a direction

of fit of mind-to-world and with a direction of causation of world-to-mind. Whether attempts to shape a church community succeed is not a matter of 'good' intentions, but a matter of suitable concrete activities. Intentions cause these activities, while activities are not determined by convictions, views or knowledge, even if these aspects may influence them.

Shaping a church community is, however, a form of collective behaviour and is, as such, not reduceable to the sum of individual activities. Searle calls collective behaviour because of its irreducability a 'primitive' phenomenon. Compare for instance, the following situations. When all people in a crowded shopping street take shelter when it suddenly rains, that is not yet 'collective behaviour.' But this would be the case when a footballteam plays a competition or when a parish counsel holds a meeting. This shows that there are at least three important differences between (the sum of) individual behaviour and collective behaviour. First of all, in collective behaviour the activities of individual members of the group refer to the activities of others. Secondly, the activities of the individual members are derived from the collective behaviour. And thirdly, the activities of the individual members usually have different contents than the collective behaviour from which they have been derived. These three characteristic features also apply to shaping a church community as collective behaviour.

To make an adequate characterisation and analysis of such behaviour, it does not suffice to add to individual intentions only mutual convictions concerning intentions and activities of others. This is currently being done in empirical approaches, but this is not right. Searle gives the example of a group of business people, who have all been trained in Adam Smith's theory of the hidden hand. Each of them believes that he may best serve the general interest when he strives after his own interests; and everyone behaves accordingly. Moreover, everyone is convinced, that the others too act according to this principle. This however, is not yet collective behaviour. There are no collective purposes or intentions. It would only become collective behaviour when these people would concur that each of them is going to help humanity by striving for his/her own personal interests. Individual activities can contribute to collective behaviour. To use the term collective behaviour is not enough for individual activities to be linked to the conviction that others also contribute to a common result. There has to be a collective purpose, and the members must be willing to achieve this goal by cooperation (Searle 1990, 404-406).

But it is a fact that collective actions are actions of individuals. And collective intentions need not be realized to be those intentions. No one can deny that. Both the intentions and their realizations do have something to do with other people. But a group, a society or a church community is exclusively made up of individuals. In a literal sense, a group-mind or a group-consciousness can never exist. A group can never be subject of anything. Strictly speaking, the church can therefore never be the subject of faith. All forms of consciousness, subjectivity or intentionality, as we know, exist only in the minds of individual people. This is also true of collective intentions. Moreover, goals or intentions are not dependent on their realization. Even when intentions do not cause the intended behaviour, they still remain the same intentions. How can these two constraints go together with the fact that collective behaviour cannot be reduced to individual behaviour? The solution to this question is, that every individual human being can have the intention to act as part of a collective body, even when others do not cooperate to achieve this collective goal.

The Structure of Collective Behaviour
For a more exact analysis of the structure of shaping the church, as collective behaviour, it is important to remember that it is composed of a mental and a physical component. Collective behaviour has this in common with every other form of intended action. The mental component is the intention to do something, the physical component is the realization of this intention in, for instance, body movements or other physical forms. As is the case with all forms of mental intentionality (e.g. perception or desires), the spiritual component represents and causes the physical component. Intentions are the mental representation of the actions, to which they are directed. If an intention is successful, the attempt to realize this intention causes the intended effect, the action carried out.

A specific feature of collective behaviour is that the mental component (the intention) itself is made up of two elements: one individual and one collective. Take for instance a footballmatch. Each of the players has the collective intention to win the game with his team. This winning is a collective element in everyone's intention. The individual singular element is different for every player. For the forward players it means kicking the ball into the goal; whereas for the goalkeeper it means stopping all balls kicked towards his goal. The individual element forms the representation of one's own contribution towards the common goal; and the collective element is the representation of the collective goal, to which they wish to contribute. Neither element can be reduced to the other. They are not two intentions which can exist apart from each other. They are two elements of one complex intention.

There have been various attempts in (ecclesiastical) political ideologies to reduce these elements to one singular intention. Collectivistic or communist ideologies try to reduce the individual element to one collective intention, but this does not administer justice to people's intentions to make an individual contribution towards the collective goal. Capitalistic or individualistic ideologies try to reduce the collective element to one individual intention. This is also unjustifiable. In that case, a person's collective intentions, which cannot be realized by his individual activities alone, are not taken seriously. The possibility of collective intentions and of collective behaviour is denied.

If the individual and collective elements within collective intentions may not be reduced to each other, the question remains as to how these elements are related to one another. Does the collective intention, for instance, cause the singular intention? This is not acceptable, since the collective intention, for instance, to win the match, is directed to a state of affairs in reality, to which the realization of the intention of the forward-player to kick the ball into the goal of the opponents, is related as means to achieve a goal. In collective behaviour it is the intention to reach the collective goal through realizing singular intentions. This complex intention causes me to realize my singular intention and this realization causes, or at least, contributes to the collective action being realized. The one complex intention, consequently, has the following structure: The collective intention B is the intention to do something by means of the realization of the individual element A. And if this collective intention succeeds, this collective intention causes A to be realized and that, because of the realization of A, B is also realized.

The Background of Collective Behaviour
All this is also valid for shaping a church community, inasfar as we may speak of collective behaviour in this matter. With a view to the possible contribution of religious socialisation to shaping a church community, it is important however, to point out something else, in the wake of Searle: collective behaviour presupposes a certain background and a certain intentional network among its participants. With 'background' Searle means all capacities, attitudes, practices, etc. that make perception, intentions and other forms of intentionality possible. By intentional network, he means that part of the background that is able to cause conscious perception, intentions and other forms of intentionality (Searle 1992, 175-196).

People can only join in collective behaviour when they have a cooperative basic attitude. They should not only judge other people as seriously as they judge themselves, but should also think others equally capable of joining in cooperation as themselves. In other words, each should think, that others can and will cooperate in realizing collective intentions. The shaping of a church community can function only against the background of such a cooperative attitude in the field of religion.

Secondly, an important precondition is that to have available the necessary know-how for cooperating with others. This background knowledge cannot, of course, consist only of know-how-it-is, but also and especially of know-how-to-do. For shaping a church community, social skills in the field of religion are important conditions.

Thirdly, collective behaviour is only possible when there is enough sense of community. This is even true of competitive and aggressive behaviour. These too, are forms of cooperation, be it on a 'higher' level. It goes without saying that not all social groups are engaged in goal-directed behaviour all the time, and consequently not always collectively. To be sure, there is always in these forms of behaviour a type of communal awareness that is the general precondition of collective intentionality. Even for the cooperation with total strangers we always need a kind of 'we-awareness'. In this case, it may take the minimal form of recognized equality. Applied to the shaping of a church community, it means that intentions to participate increase proportionately to the religious we-awareness.

Therefore, it is incorrect to found the community on communication, as is often done now – especially, according to Habermas and Apel, – also where the church and the shaping of the church community are concerned. The reverse is more true, namely that communication is based on community. Communication is also a form of collective behaviour. It is also made possible by a sense of community. And a lack of a community sense hinders the communication. Society, community or church cannot be explained in terms of communication or collective behaviour in general, for these presuppose a form of living together and cooperation before they can function at all.

This does not mean that furthering religious communication within the framework of shaping a church community is not important. Nor does it imply that a training in collective activity, such as religious communication, could not contribute to the sense of community, the social skills and the cooperative frame of mind which are necessary for shaping a church community. Elements having a logical priority need not necessarily come chronologically or psychologically first. In St. Paul's time, christian communities were born and grew in and through communication (Reck, 1991). In a context marked by individualisation and decline of church membership, it is obvious to attach great importance, within the bounds of practical theology and religious education of religion, to (promoting) religious communication. Training in religious communication may form an important part of religious socialisation and may thus play an important role in developing a religious sense of community, of religious-social skills and of a cooperative attitude in the field of religion. But we must realize, that this background is elementary, when a church community is to be shaped at all.

As long as religious socialisation does not contribute more to this, it cannot contribute to furthering a church community.

2. The Socialisation of a Reduced Faith

During the last decades the teaching of religion has pursued paths that have scarely allowed it to pay attention to these collective aspects and preconditions for shaping a church community. This is not only due to 'external' causes of a general social nature, such as secularisation and individualisation of faith, religion and 'Weltanschauung', but especially by the internal development of (practical theological) study of religious education. This recent development arose as an explicit reaction to the transfer of faith in the first half of the twentieth century, in particular to its heteronomic character: others, especially the ecclesiastical authorities, decreed what people had to believe and how they ought to live in accordance with this faith. People have, since the sixties, strongly protested against this kind of transfer of faith. And in a reaction to this, people who taught the subject of religion, began to search for a form of religious education that would further people's religious and philosophical autonomy. This, at any rate, seems to me to be the most dominant trend inherited from the sixties.

The Individualistic Reduction
In a first phase people have reacted against the ecclesiastical collectivism, that typified the religious socialisation during the first half of this century. This collectivism thought it sufficient when people shared a common faith and experienced this faith as the church decreed. It took neither personal intention, nor personel conviction, nor individual elements in the collective faith into consideration. It left the believer's individual intention to contribute in their own way to collective intentions out of its consideration and did not explain how the church's faith could move people to contribute personally to common goals, such as a shared experience of faith. This ecclesiastical collectivism was usually coupled with religious formalism and with an objectification of 'the' faith, in which the subjective aspects of the act of faith were neglected. In a reaction to this, people in the sixties and seventies pleaded for a drastic change in religious education: this education ought to take its origin from the student's experiences and should be directed to the development of a personal attitude of faith.

One example of this approach is Halbfas' proposed 'revision of religious education' (Halbfas, 1972a, 1972b and 1974). In this proposal he criticizes the traditional christian ecclesiastical practice of education, originating from a concept of religion that sharply contrasts with institutional religiosity. He describes real religion as an attitude of man who he asks questions rising above himself and the factual state of affairs. It is 'the deepest force of man, with which he asks in all his forms of expression for the whence and the purpose of life, society and world' (Halbfas 1972a,5).

According to Halbfas every human being is potentially religious, if only he is willing to accept everything that renders sense to human life. Religious education must, therefore, be based on this general human basis. 'By religious education we mean the education towards a fully developed open humanity, which asks from above itself and therein escapes from every ideological narrowing, even when such an openness takes away all would-be security and leads to a way, behind which there seems to be no more home. The tasks of the religious education fit, therefore, within the tasks of a general human education, but do not completely exhaust themselves in this way. Because religiosity is not an exceptional gift of people, but belongs to the spiritual, original capacity of man, in which he tries to understand himself, religious education means an opening up of man for his deepest capacity, victory over self-alienation and a help to finding oneself' (Halbfas 1972a,9). It precedes christian or any other confessional education, at least in a logical sense, not necessarily in a chronological sense.

If we compare traditional christian education with this understanding of religion and with the understanding of religious education which is based on it, we must, according to Halbfas conclude, that this makes man unreligious, inasfar as children are given answers before forming their own questions; inasfar as they are made dependent on certainties, which later appear unsatisfactory and inasfar as they are given to understand contents which, in our presentday world, prove to be mostly empty formulas. Opposite these extremely empty formulas, Halbfas places education in a positive religiosity. In his understanding religion and finding one's identity are necessarily a programme, in which religion does not lose itself, but addresses our primary concern: man's becoming a human being.

Religious education is not the recruitment for an established religion, nor preparation for traditions that have become irreligious. It is the coming into being of religion itself. It does not strive for anything specific, but for the whole agreement of man with the truth, which carries him with his identity.

The fundamental principle of such a religious education, the education to determine one's own self, is according to Halbfas realized in three postulates:

1. children must be enabled to express their needs freely, without restraint and must be able to regulate them themselves;
2. children must be able to learn to investigate reality and test it;
3. children must learn to judge all decisions and acts in their social consequences, but should be spared a 'morality-of-the-way-things-are-

100

done' which makes it impossible for them to find their own identity. Halbfas evidently concludes, that the child is a self-regulating, tendentious autonomous being. And he criticizes institutions by an understanding of rules, which he links to the individual development of every human being (Morgenthaler 1976, 87-88).

We see this same approach in many other religious educators in the sixties and early seventies, but usually less radical than with Halbfas, often with different emphases, yet with the same basic tones. In the Netherlands, for instance, the so-called 'experience-catechesis', which became quite popular in catholic circles, is a clear exponent of this approach. Its most valuable point is its justified emphasis on faith, religion and 'Weltanschauung' depending on the inalienable spiritual directions and capacities of the individual people. This reaction to the church's collectivism, however, went one step further. People took the individual directiveness not only to be a direction of individuals, but also as a direction for the actions and of states of affairs important to those individuals. The collective element of collective intentions and of collective convictions, memories and experiences was reduced to the individual element. It was denied collective intentionality fits in the domain of religion. The starting point was a false dilemma: either faith as an individual mental intentionality to the deepest inner self of the singular man, or meaningless collective formal rules of the groups without faith. Given this dilemma, people evidently considered it necessary to eliminate the second element in religious education as much as possible, and to give as many chances as possible to the first element. They reduced faith to strictly personal experiences, convictions and intentions. All forms of religious behaviour were reduced to individual activities. Nothing was left of the collective behaviour, needed to shape a church community. The importance of shaping a church community was not denied. But it was taken for granted that this was not caused by the collective intentions of people, but that the individual intention of people to experience their own faith in a personal manner – knowing that others too experience their own faith – would lead to the build up of a church community. Religious socialisation's contribution to shaping a church community was limited to socialisation. People tried to help develop individual intentions and convictions in the field of religion.

The Cognitivistic Reduction
Partly as a reaction to this approach, a second phase in development in present day religious education has risen since the early seventies. It became increasingly clear that the loosening ties between individual and community advocated in the previous phase was not realistic. The second phase emphasised the interaction of individual and community recognizing that the

influence of the individual person's context is not always favourable to his development. Moreover, it argued that this 'anti-social' ideologisation of christianity was in many cases connected to a religious emotivism and a functionalisation of christian faith for the interests of well-to-do citizens in church and society. That is why it was argued that religious education should allow teachers to think critically about the religious dimension of reality using theologically justified conceptual structures. The individual should be armed against alienating influences from church and society. A balance should be formed between the many environmental influences and the individual's identity.

A good example of this second phase is Reiser's use of symbolic interactionism in his book 'Identität und religiöse Einstellung' (Reiser 1972). Reiser starts from a different understanding of religion than Halbfas. Like Luckmann, he sees religion as a worldview, an outlook on the world. He describes religion 'as a complex of institutions and patterns of interpretation regarding an unconditional sense of life, which are acquired during the process of socialisation (Reiser 1972, 22). He does not start from two forms of religion, like Halbfas. He distinguishes between two opposite 'workings' of religion: one furthering identity and one hindering identity. By identity he means, like Erikson, Goffmann and Habermas, the confirmation of the unity of the self in material space (physical 'I') in the social space (social identity) and in duration (personal identity). This I-identity is threatened by both finiteness, which ends the continuity of the I in space and time, and by the infiniteness, which destroys the scheme of space-time, which the I constitutes. The I creates, by the negation of finiteness, the idea of infiniteness, but at the same time tries to reinsert it into the space-time-scheme through magical manipulations. Here lies man's paradoxal existence. Religion acquired in socialisation supplies patterns, however, which people may use to control paradoxal existence be it in a progressive or regressive sense. Irrational patterns tend to ward off the paradox and shield the I against contradictory experiences of inner and outer reality. With rational patterns man may, however, conquer contradictions. It is interesting that Reiser thinks it important that rationality of sense makes social engagement possible. He considers social engagement to be a 'generalisation of a socially felt integrity and autonomy of the I in relation to humanity and its history' (Reiser 1972, 22).

Religious education should, according to Reiser, minimize the identity-smothering effect of religion and increase its stimulating effect upon identity. He emphasises that rational schemes can only be acquired, when a person experiences security, autonomy and solidarity in socialisation. This presupposes, that the repressive, rigid and behaviour-controlling aspects of education are witheld; that the childs needs are recognized; and that the will to direct oneself and the formation of one's self is being stimulated. Such an education can only be realized under different social conditions. Christianity would have to give up its magic veiling of the dialectics of existence and its function to stabilize power in favour of a new understanding of faith.

Reiser investigates empirically, which religious institutions have a stimulating or an inhibiting effect on the I-strength of young people. He distinguishes between I-weak and I-strong tendencies in religious statements expressed in certain forms of judgement. The I-strong personality is, according to Reiser, typified by the choice of critical-logical, identity involved and altruistic judgments. The I-weak is typified by a choice for pseudo-rational, emotional, heteronome, egoistic and magical judgments. A pedagogically desirable attitude toward statements concerning faith is, according to him, an attitude determined by I-strong tendencies. Attitudes determined by rejecting tendencies are pedagogically undesirable. From his research for the various dimensions of religious attitudes, he concludes that agreement with statements on christian faith is equal to fear of punishment, to social desirability, social rigidity and desintegration of groups. Agreement and rejection of faith may both be the result of both I-strong and I-weak motives.

According to Reiser, the results of his research form a back-up for a religious education that looks critically at the religion of young people, that halts to heteronomic and egoistical agreement to faith, that analyses the rejection of faith determined by feeling and pseudo-rational considerations, and that is not afraid of aggressive expression (Reiser 1972, 77). He pleads for a religious education that corrects a failed process of finding one's identity by assimilating conflict in group-processes. The theme has to be 'the religion of the pupils'. Students should be helped to control their fate via socialisation. This invalues eliminating socially damaging religious attitudes. It also invalues a critical-logical attitude towards the problem of human identity. We should learn to bear the dialectics of our existence. Education should observe carefully, according to Freud's scheme of remembering, repeating and processing, how to enlist the state of the students' problems and to assimilate the resistance and forms of transmission. 'The starting point is always a certain set of problems that influence the pupils who live these problems or deny them. It is our goal to encourage a group-process using the subject matter, one that calls unconscious images, analyses and processes to memory' (Reiser 1972, 105). All subject-matter is suitable that appeals to the pupil's problem, that starts a process of clearing up and that has been tested in a 'dynamic-didactical analysis' for its suitability for such education (Morgenthaler, 1976, 165-167).

We observed this approach in many religious educationists during the seventies and in the early eighties, although it has been worked out in different ways. Some, following Habermas, start from a negative dialectics between the individual and the group. They share with others a strong emphasis on the individual's historical-social and physical situation and the desire to pay attention to the influence of that context on the individual and on the individual's intentionality. A personal faith never develops apart from a present context. This faith may obtain a certain significance and function of which we should be particulary critical. This is the most valuable point in the approach. This reaction to the ideological character of religious education tends to overreach. One does not confine itself to breaking the individual and group apart, but puts them opposite each other. People acknowledge that the collective group influences the individual, but not that the individual influences the collective group.

The individual's intentionality towards his 'Umwelt' is reduced to 'cognitive' intentionality, to intentionality with a mind-to-world direction of fit and, consequently with a world-to-mind direction of causation. For Reiser it becomes evident that religion is a way of looking at the world expressed in positive and negative judgments about religious statements. These are typical assertions: presentations of intentional states with a world-to-mind direction of causation. The same is evident from terminology like 'rendering sense' and 'patterns of interpretation'. That religion may also contain intentions or desires, for instance the intention to improve with others certain things in the world, remains out of scope, or is reduced to accepting or rejecting such an 'idea'. The individual's convictions relating to the group or to values and standards alive in the group are usually restricted to convictions relating to the individual itself. The group's influence on the individual only touches the individual and his identity, not the group. Reiser's standard of social engagement does not alter this. This engagement is, according to him, merely a generalisation of the individual's unassailableness and independency as opposed to humanity and its history. The reduction of the collective group to the individual is pushed to extremes. It is made legal and valid for all people. This tendency to reduce all mental states to 'cognitive' intentionality with a direction of causation of world-to-mind, results in the radical reduction of the collective to the individual element in collective forms of intentionality.

Little remained of practical participation in shaping a church community. The importance of shaping a church community was not denied, yet it was not considered a purpose of religious education, but merely as one possible result. Van der Ven, in his 'Katechetische leerplanontwikkeling', calls shaping the church community an intrinsic tendency (Van der Ven, 1973, 150). This means implicitly that individual cognitive intentionality (knowledge and faith) was not considered as sufficient, but was the most important condition for shaping a church community. This is a further form of an individualistic solution to the problem of collective intentions. The starting point is no longer that people's individual intentions to experience their own faith personally – knowing that others too experience their own faith – will lead to shaping a church community. The starting point is now that individual knowledge and religious convictions may result in shaping a church community. The only possible contribution religious socialisation made to shaping a church community was the formation of individual cognitive intentionality: knowledge, understanding, convictions and thoughts. Van der Ven calls this 'the development of a critically differentiated ecclesiastical self-image', Van der Ven 1982, 443.

The Materialistic Reduction

A third phase takes another step forward. Previously religion took its contents from christianity. For an increasing number of religious educationists this could not continue given the religious pluralism in our society. In the eighties a new approach was developed, which received a new name in Holland. People no longer spoke of religious or spiritual education, but of 'levensbe-schouwelijke vorming' (philosophical training). This third phase not only radically reduced the collective to the individual element, but also more radically reduced intentions to cognitive forms of intentionality. This did not happen on purpose. It was the consequence of a growing resistance to the preference for christianity. People emphasized the individual's freedom to choose among available philosophies of life. The individual must first understand what an 'attitude to life' is, if he is to understand specific contents of each. Religious education was to make young people sophisticated enough in the field of 'Weltanschauung' to make their own responsible choices.

One example of this phase's effects on religious education is Van der Ven's and Rijksen's theory of the coordination of perspectives (Van der Ven 1984 and Rijksen 1984). Using this theory, Van der Ven tried to solve the problem of how far the contents of religious education may and must be derived from theology or religious sciences. Rijksen applied the same theory to more practical problems of how justice can be done, within religious education, to both the pupils' convictions and the convictions of those who are of another opinion and how these two can be combined fruitfully. The theory says: In communication there are three possible perspectives: the I-, the you- and the he- or it-perspective. Every human being observes reality from his own angle. When making or interpreting a statement, one communicates from the I-perspective. For a fruitful dialogue, this is not enough. We must try to place ourselves in the position of the other. This is called decentralisation.

Instead of speaking and interpreting out of one's own point of view, this is done from the point of view of the debating partner. For me, someone else's viewpoint is a you-perspective, just as my point of view is for somebody else. The I-perspective and the you-perspective may differ or be opposed to each other. To control these differences or contrasts, we need to coordinate perspectives. This implies considering statements from the I-perspective and statements from the you-perspective from a more abstract perspective as species of a genus. Then we may speak of a he-, she- or it-perspective. The I-perspective becomes coordinated with the you-perspective. From this point, agreements and differences between the former statements can be discussed and reinterpreted, allowing dialogue to develop further. During the dialogue the discussing partners can develop themselves further. They may learn something from others, if they are able to change perspectives regularly. As we stated before, this theory has been applied in different ways to the dialogue with or between people having various religions and attitudes to life. By the I-perspective they mean for instance the personal vision of the teachers, such as the christian theological viewpoint. The you-perspective is the point of view, in the same aspect, of everyone else except the teacher himself or of non-christian theologians. The core of the matter in the educational process, or in teaching, is that teachers first endeavour to become conscious of and express their own (christian) point of view. Consequently, they have to put themselves into the you-perspective of the others. They have to learn to consider themselves from a distance, as the center from which they look at reality, to think and feel as others would. They must learn to take over the roles of the others and defend their arguments from that perspective. Finally, they should compare both conceptions by taking a he-, she- or it-perspective, raising both to a higher level of abstraction, to connect the two.

According to Van der Ven, this perspective typifies religious sciences. When they then have returned to their own theological point of view, adapting it to what they have learned from others, the circle of changing coordinating perspective may begin anew so that the process of learning may continue. Neither, Van der Ven and Rijksen, starts from different kinds of religiosity or from different effects of religion, but from different concepts of the attitude towards life by different people from various backgrounds.

This is only one of the many attempts, in this third phase of the present, to take seriously and recognize people in our society, who have other ways of thinking or to take the pluralism in the 'Weltanschauung'. This is a valuable element recognizing the pupil's freedom to choose an attitude towards life. It is less positive, that the reduction of collective convictions and intentions to individual forms of intentionality, which was radicalized already in the previous phase, is driven to extremes in this phase. This is done in three ways. First, one is not restricted to freeing the individual from the collective group, nor even to a contrast between the two. The collective group is merged into individuals. In the theory of the change-of-perspective, there is only an I, a you and a he, but no we. Collective groups contain nothing but the sumtotal of individuals. Second, one reason this happens is that all forms of intentionality are thoroughly reduced to 'cognitive' intentional states. In the theory of the coordination of perspectives intentions to communicate are reduced to the points of view, perspectives or convictions being communicated. This happens in a way which is just as subtle as it is fateful. In the third and complete reduction of collective intentions, all intrinsic mental states are reduced to observer-relative ascriptions of intentionality or to observer-relative ascriptions of functions to their mental states. Accordingly, in this theory, in the he-, she- or in the it-perspective, we must adapt the point of view of the observer. We should thus attribute something shared to ourselves and to our discussion partner. The significance of this attribution is determined from its it-perspective. Both opinions or intrinsic intentionalities are thus reduced to an observer-relative ascription of intentionality. Moreover, we must realise that this theory is based on the assumption, that I as an individual, take all three points of view consecutively. In this way the intentionality of others is first reduced to my intentionality and, next, both intrinsic mental states are being reduced to observer-relative ascriptions of intentionality, to observable behaviour. All experiences, memories, religious convictions, views etc. are reduced to meanings, which observers attribute to perceptable behaviour in the field of religion. Consequently, nothing is left of a contribution to the shape of a church community as something, that people themselves wanted or within which their own faith played a role. Although the importance of shaping a church community is not denied, it is not a possible effect or purpose of religious education. At best, the subject church – the relations between church and pupil and between churches and society – is considered a theme within religious education since the life of the church is an important phenomenon in the field of 'Weltanschauung'. All that remains of religious socialisation's role in shaping a church community is its attempt to develop an observer of the church.

Sometimes it seems as if there is a new phase. The dilemma heteronomy – autonomy, which dominated the whole development as described, seems to be under control in communicative religious education where Habermas' 'intersubjective' theory of communication is an important source of inspiration. Yet Habermas and the theory of symbols have not effected this triple reduction. For here the communication of intrinsic intentions of faith is reduced to observer-relative ascription of conviction and functions to perceptable 'religious' behaviour. This reduction in the present-day religious education learnes little of intrinsic faith other than individual convictions, memories and perceptions which 'observers' ascribe to people, whether they are circumscribed in terms of 'rendering sense', 'attitude to life' or 'answer to questions of life'. Hardly any room has been left for a theory of or an investigation into collective intentions in the field of religion, as intrinsic intentionality. This way of teaching religion today can no longer find an answer to the question of how religious socialisation can contribute to shaping a church community as collective behaviour.

3. Towards a Cooperative Religious Education

To find a satisfactory answer to this question religious education should take a new direction where the reductions mentioned above are avoided or controlled, while retaining the acquirements from the recent developments. And the religious education may not fall back into a heteronome form of the transmission of faith. These three conditions could be met, if religious education has been developed in an explicitly cooperative direction, and if we look for a solution in that direction for the problem of a possible contribution of religious socialisation to shaping a church community. Let me detail the basic lines of that solution.

Our Intrinsic Faith
First, we should look at how religious education could stimulate intrinsic faith without a reduction, but also without force and with a recognition of the difference.

Religious education should start from a non-materialistic solution to the body-mind problem. The reduction of intrinsic intentionality to observer-relative ascriptions is based on a materialistic reduction of mental states and events to physical processes such as the functioning of the brain and the central nervous system. But religious education should not be reduced to mentalism or another form of dualism.

It should take as its starting-point,
* that people have mental states, or that mental processes may occur (e.g. religious faith or the desire for a joint experience of faith)
* that these states and processes are not reducible to physical events (the working of the brain or going to church)
* that they are caused by physical features and processes (the working of the brain) and
* that they are realized in physical events (going to church) (comp. Searle,

108

1984).

Using this starting-point, religious education may study the intrinsic faith of young people and their willingness to join in activities, that further a joint experience of faith. Religious education may also look for possibilities to stimulate children and young people to develop their own intrinsic faith. This is obviously the first and most fundamental condition for joining in shaping a church community. As long as people remain mere observers of faith and the experience of faith, they cannot participate in shaping a church community, however responsibly and cleverly they may, from this point of view of observers, ascribe meaning to faith and church. Of course, this intrinsic faith may not be an imposed faith, realized under force. But freedom of religion does not mean choosing from available religious convictions. It means believing from free will. This free, personal faith, need not stand apart from or be opposed to the faith that people share with each other. Intrinsic faith does not oppose collective faith, but opposes the ascription of faith.

To do justice to another's intrinsic faith, religious education must adopt a manner of acquiring knowledge that agrees with the above solution of the body-mind-problem. It may not be a purely objectivating method, which tries to approach the intrinsic mental states of people, from a so-called 3rd person point of view. This would use the acquisition of knowledge to reduce intrinsic mental states to observer-relative ascriptions of faith or other mental states. The 3rd person point of view is always an observer's 1st person point of view, not a participant's. Yet religious education may not become subjectivistic or regress to another form of acquiring knowledge not open to public questioning.

Religious educationists should accept:
* that people know best what goes on in their minds, for instance their own faith;
* that they are best equipped to tell this to others;
* that the acquisition of knowledge is best done consciously and critically, and
* that the acquisition of knowledge accurs best in recognition and analysis of what the others express about this themselves.

These rules are also valid when investigating religious education, for instance, when examining how far the religious socialisation contributes to the preparedness and ability of young people to participate in activities that promote a joint experience of faith. With a view to shaping a church community, religious education should primarily use these rules to help young people learn to understand better the intrinsic faith of others. We do not mean adopting someone else's faith nor taking someone else's place even temporarily, but understanding in the sense of recognition. This recognition of what others believe is a second important condition for participating in shaping a church society on a free basis while retaining autonomy.

A precondition for recognizing another's intrinsic faith without reduction and for the development of personal intrinsic faith during religious socialisation is a non-solistic, cooperative religious orientation. In developing this, religious socialisation may contribute to shaping a church community. Only with this attitude can people be sure that they express their thoughts successfully. Yet religious education should not be merely an attitude in which one's own faith – even temporarily – is ignored. Religious education should be aware:

* that people recognize other people as being equally important as themselves in the field of religion and life-attitudes;
* that people experience another's presence as a potential opportunity for cooperation in the field of religion and 'Weltanschauung', and
* that people may therefore engage in collective behaviour such as activities that promote a communal experience of faith.

People need not deny their own faith nor see the personal faith of others as a threat to their own faith. It is important for religious education to accept that the people with different faiths may work together.

Capable of Action and Emotion

Religious education should also look for opportunities to further intrinsic faith that also contain intended activities and emotions not reduced to 'cognitive' intentionality. These intentions and emotions must withstand the test of (ideology-) criticism and be rationally responsible.

For that reason religious education must start from a non-externalistic solution of the problem of how mental states relate to reality. The reduction of all mental states to 'cognitive' intentionality, to intentional states with a mind-to-world direction of fit, is based on the incorrect externalistic opinion that human representations of reality do not suffice to determine the contents and the identity of various religions convictions, intentions, etc., but that these contents and identity are always determined by contextual, causal conditions in the world. Religious education must guard against context-free internalism, as if people's background and intentional network could exert no influence on the nature and the contents of their mental states. It must therefore bear in mind:

* that mental states directed towards an object, a state of affairs or an event contain a mental representation of the matter that is required when this conviction will be true, this intention realised or that desire granted. Intentional states must contain a representation of their 'conditions of satisfaction'.
* that those mental states may differ inasfar as the conditions of satisfaction

they represent have a direction of fit of mind-to-world (perception, memories and convictions) or of world-to-mind (intentions, plans and desires); that intentionality with a given direction of fit consequently cannot be reduced to intentionality with a reverse direction of fit;

* that emotions have no direction of fit, because even emotions, which are directed to something (for instance fear for something) are already presupposed, to contain a correspondence between the propositional contents of this intentionality and the state of affairs in the reality these contents represent; that therefore, emotions cannot be reduced to 'cognitions' in the sense of intentionality with a mind-to-world direction of fit.

Given this relationship of mental states to the world, it is important not only to do research, within the study of religious education, on the influence leading to religious convictions or other 'cognitive' intentionality within the religious socialisation, but also on the influence leading to religious desires, intentions and emotions. With a view to religious socialisation's contribution to shaping a church community, religious education should look for opportunities to develop, within the faith of children and young people, not only a personal network of convictions, memories and perception-experiences in the field of religion, but also a network of desires, plans, intentions and emotions. These should withstand the criticism of ideology. This need not mean that religious education is restricted to thinking critically.

To do justice to the significance of the intentions of communicative actions, religious education should be based upon a logical explanation of these intentions. They should agree with the solution of the relation-problem between mind and world. Consequently, this may not be a purely propositional logic restricting the logical status and properties of mental states to the propositional content of judgments or equating the meaning of communicative actions to the claims for their validity. To do so would be using 'logic', to reduce the meaning-intentions of our and others' communicative actions to intentional states with a mind-to-world direction of fit. These so-called validity claims are always judgments about propositional content, their truth, correctness or sincerity. The performance of a communicative action that commits the speaker to the conditions belonging to a succesful performance of this action should not be confused with the assertion that these communitative actions necessitate an attempt to convince the listener to agree with the speakers' validity claims. Of course, communication works best when there is a spirit of cooperation between speaker and listener. The speaker will then try to reach a consensus with the listener, for instance by acknowledging his straight-forwardness, or by consenting to his justification for the communicative action concerned. But it is a mistake to suppose that the features of a succesful cooperation and communication are part of a definition of meaning.

People can, doubtless, communicate meaningfully without agreeing on validity claims; but religious education may not sink to irrationality or a form of invalid 'logic'.

Religious education should bear in mind:

* that intensional forms of intentionality, i.e. directedness to intentional states, may not be confused with the mental states to which they are directed;
* that intensionality always has a mind-to-world direction, because they are 'reports' of mental states, whereas the mental states themselves may also have a world-to-mind direction (e.g. intentions) or have no direction of fit at all (e.g. emotions);
* that it is logically relevant whether reports of mental states also repeat the propositional content of those mental states, committing the thinker to the contents;
* that it, logically, is even more relevant whether these reports contain a repetition of the whole mental state committing the person whose directedness it is to this mental state.

These differences in logical status must also be taken into account in the research into religious education as in the inquiry into the contribution of religious socialisation to the participation of young people in activities that will further a joint experience of faith. In that inquiry we may not restrict the meaning of statements on religion to the propositional contents of reports or judgments about those statements. As to shaping a church community, religious education should look for opportunities, not only to teach young people how to judge, reason or debate about faith and statements about faith, but also to teach them to communicate their own intrinsic faith, express their emotions and non-cognitive intentional states and understand what others mean to say. A precondition for this logical communication of non-cognitive elements in the network of one's own faith is a skill not restricted to knowing-how-it-is but open to a knowing-how-to-do, a skill in communicating intrinsic faith. Religious socialisation may thus contribute in an important way to shaping a church community. This skill gives meaning to intentions and actions as much as to 'cognitions' and facts. Only so are people able to act in a rational way. Yet more is needed than a mere separation between theoretical and practical 'background knowledge'.

Religious education should take into account in the subject of religion:

* that there is no action without perception, nor perception without action;
* that the forms of intentionality occur within a coordinated flow of actions and observations, and that the background-skill is, theoretically and practically, the condition of possibility for the forms, which this flow adopts;
* that mental aims tend to reach the level of background faculties.

It is relevant to shaping a church community that religious socialisation develops practical religious skill without requirring students always to act religiously or having to express their faith. Some training in this respect is a precondition for any desired action.

With Collective Elements

Finally, religious education should concern itself primarily with promoting intrinsic faith, including collective behaviour. This behaviour must be personal, in the sense of wanting to act from the depth of one's heart. To realize this, religious education should start from a non-individualistic solution to the problem, of how individual intentions can be directed to behaviour irreducible to the behaviour of individuals. The reduction of collective intentions to individual intentions is based on the individualistic reduction of one person's intentions to the intentions to act in an individual way. On the other hand religious education should not be reduced to collectivism.

Therefore its starting-point should be:
* that collective intentions too, are intentional states of individual people;
* that these intentions are composed of an individual and a collective element, and
* that both elements are related to each other as means to end.

On the basis of this structure-analysis of collective intentions it is important, not only to do research inside religious education, into the influences of religious socialisation on the individual behaviour of people, but also into its influence on their collective behaviour. With a view to the possible contribution of religious socialisation to shaping a church community, religious education should look for opportunities to help young people come to collective intentions in the field of religion. These must be personal intentions supported by personal experiences of actions. Religious education need not, however, be restricted to developing intentions in the field of religion.

Community sense is a precondition for developing these collective intentions without reduction. This is the most important, but also the most difficult requirement to avoid or surmount the reduction of collective intentions to individual intentions. Yet within the context of individualisation and decline of church membership it is necessary to develop this sense of community in the religious socialisation, if it is to contribute to shaping a church community. Without such a purposeful mind it is impossible to want to realize goals together with others that are of greater importance than the personal activities that contribute to them. Yet religious education should not deteriorate into a religious communism. It should have as a starting point:
* that individual people may also realize in the field of religion and in their

attitudes to life, that they are not alone, but belong to a community;
* that this communal awareness is not a conscious conviction, but a matter of course, and
* that we can distinguish various levels of community sense.

Religious education should consider which level of community sense religious socialisation has as its goal in the present context. Regarding its contribution to shaping a church community, it should look for opportunities to use religious socialisation to develop a sense of community, without a permanent consensus or identical set of goals.

Community in that case means a union of cooperation and a communion of communication, communio in the sense of team and togetherness, not uniformity or complete agreement. Religious education need not be completely determined by individualisation and decline of church membership, but it may also contribute to an urgently necessary renewed society.

Literature

ANDREE, T., P. STEEGMAN (red.), Religieuze socialisatie, Utrecht 1987

ARGYLE, M., Cooperation. The Basis of Sociability, London/New York 1991

ARNDT, M. (Hrsg.), Religiöse Sozialisation, Stuttgart 1975

BAART, A., B. HÖFTE (red.) Betrokken hemel, betrokken aarde. Naar een praktische theologie van lokale kerkopbouw, Baarn 1994

BECKER, J., R. VINK, Secularisatie in Nederland 1966-1991: de verandering van opvattingen en enkele sociale gedragingen, Sociaal en Cultureel Planbureau, Rijswijk 1994

ESTER, P., L. HALMAN, R. DE MOOR, The Individualizing Society: Value Change in Europe and North America, Tilburg 1993

GEURTS, T., A. DE JONG, Naar een kommunikatieve katechese, Themanummer Verbum 1986, 7/8

HALBFAS, H., Revision der religiösen Erziehung, in: Informationen zum Religionsunterricht, 1972 (a), Heft 1, 44 a.f.

HALBFAS, H., Revision der religiösen Erziehung II, in: Informationen zum Religionsunterricht, 1972 (b), Heft 3, 1 a.f.

HALBFAS, H., Revision der religiösen Erziehung III, in: Informationen zum Religionsunterricht, 1974, Heft 3, 23 a.f.

HEMERT, M. VAN, Kunnen kerken leren omgaan met de toenemende individualisering? in: Een-twee-een, jrg. 22 n.4. (18 maart 1994)

HURRELMANN, K., D. ULICH (Hrsg.), Handbuch der Sozialisationsforschung, Weinheim/Basel 1980

HÜNERMANN, P., R.SCHAEFFLER (Hrsg.), Theorie der Sprachhandlungen und heutige Ekklesiologie (QD 109), Freiburg i. Br. 1987

JONG, A. DE, Weerklank van Job. Over geloofstaal in bijbellessen, Kampen 1990

KUHNKE, U., Koinonia. Zur theologischen Rekonstruktion der Identität christlicher Gemeinde, Düsseldorf 1992

LANGE, F. DE, Ieder voor zich? Individualisering, ethiek en christelijk geloof, Kampen 1993

LEPORE, E., R. VAN GULICK (Ed.), John Searle and his Critics, Cambridge 1992

METTE, N., Voraussetzungen christlicher Elementarerziehung. Vorbereitende Studien zu einer Religionspädagogik des Kleinkindalters, Düsseldorf 1983

MORGENTHALER, C., Sozialisation und Religion. Sozialwissenschaftliche Materialien zur religionspädagogischen Theoriebildung, Gütersloh 1976

RECK, R., Kommunikation und Gemeindeaufbau. Eine Studie zu Entstehung, Leben und Wachstum paulinischer Gemeinden in den Kommunikationsstrukturen der Antike, Stuttgart 1991

REISER, H., Identität und religiöse Einstellung, Hamburg 1972

RIJKSEN, H., A. VAN REISEN, Een bijdrage aan het dialoogmodel binnen het godsdienstonderwijs, in: Verbum 1984, nr. 4, 143-163

SEARLE, J.R., Minds, Brains and Science, Cambridge 1984

SEARLE, J.R., Collective Intentions and Actions, in: P.R.Cohen e.o. (Ed.), Intentions in Communication, Cambridge 1990, 401-415

SEARLE, J.R., The Rediscovery of Mind, Cambridge/London 1992

VEN, J.A. VAN DER, Katechetische leerplanontwikkeling, Den Bosch 1973

VEN, J.A. VAN DER, Godsdienstwetenschap of theologie: een vals dilemma in de godsdienstpedagogiek, in: Verbum 1984 nr.5, 170-197

VEN, J.A. VAN DER, Kritische godsdienstdidactiek, Kampen 1982

VEN, J.A. VAN DER, Ecclesiologie in context, Kampen 1993

Contributors

Ernest Henau C.P. (Erwetegem, Belgium, 1937) is Professor in Pastoral Theology at Catholic University of Nijmegen and Director of the Flemish Catholic Broadcasting Corporation (KTRO) in Brussels.

Chis Hermans (Rucphen, the Netherlands, 1955) is Dr.Theol. and Professor in the service of the Catholic University of Nijmegen. Teaching commitment: Foundations and identity of Catholic religious education.

Aad de Jong (Noord-Scharwoude, the Netherlands, 1943) is Dr.Theol. and Senior Teacher in Pastoral Theology at the Catholic University of Nijmegen and Coordinator of the University Centre for Theological and Pastoral Studies (U.T.P.) in Heerlen.

Robert J. Schreiter C.Pp.S. (Nebraska City, USA, 1947) is Professor of Historical and Doctrinal Studies at Catholic Theological Union in Chicago. He is editor of the 'Orbis – Faith and Culture' series.

Johannes A. van der Ven (Breda, the Netherlands, 1940) is Professor in Practical Theology at the Catholic University of Nijmegen and holds a named professorship in St. Paul University, Ottawa, Canada. He is editor of the 'Journal of Empirical Theology'.

Hans-Georg Ziebertz (D-Alpen, Deutschland, 1956) is Dr. rer. soc. and habil. theol.. He is University Teacher in Empirical Theology and Religious Pedagogics in the Catholic University of Nijmegen.

Theologie & Empirie

1. J.A. van der Ven (red.), Pastoraal tussen ideaal en werkelijkheid, Kampen, 1985.
2. H.J.M. Vossen, Vrijwilligerseducatie en pastoraat aan rouwenden. Een pastoraaltheologisch onderzoek naar een curriculum voor vrijwilligers in het pastoraat over het bijstaan van rouwenden, Kampen, 1985.
3. G.T. van Gerwen, Catechetische begeleiding. Een onderzoek naar het effect van een educatieprogramma voor onderwijsgevenden aan het basisonderwijs, Kampen, 1985.
4. C.A.M. Hermans. Morele vorming. Empirisch-theologisch onderzoek naar de effecten van een katechese-curriculum in de morele vorming omtrent de milieucrisis, Kampen, 1986.
5. J.A.M. Siemerink, Het gebed in de religieuze vorming. Empirisch-theologisch onderzoek naar de effecten van gebedseducatie bij volwassenen, Kampen, 1987.
6. M.P.J. van Knippenberg, Dood en religie. Een studie naar communicatief zelfonderzoek in het pastoraat, Kampen, 1987.
7. G.T. van Gerwen, Pastorale begeleiding door vrijwilligers. Empirisch-theologisch onderzoek naar de motivatie tot deelname aan pastorale zorg in levenscrises, Kampen, 1990.
8. A.Th.M. de Jong, Weerklank over Job. Over geloofstaal in bijbellessen, Kampen, 1990.
9. H.-G. Ziebertz, Moralerziehung im Wertpluralismus. Eine empirisch-theologische Untersuchung nach moralpädagogischen Handlungskonzepten im Religionsunterricht und in der kirchlichen Jugendarbeit zu Fragen der Sexualität, Kampen/Weinheim, 1990.

Herausgegeben von
H.F. Rupp, A.H.M. Scheer, J.A. van der Ven, H.-G. Ziebertz.